Forging History

The story of George Barnsley & Sons, toolmakers
*and the many family members who helped to
forge local and national history*

Pauline Bell with Colin Barnsley

ISBN: 978-1-906722-16-6

To contact:
Colin Barnsley
George Barnsley & Sons Ltd
C/O Woodware Repetitions Ltd
47 Mowbray Street
Sheffield S3 8EN
0114 272 6060
email: cjbarnsley@hotmail.com

Pauline Bell
pbell7@btinternet.com

Foreword

It is a great pleasure to endorse this history of the family and company of George Barnsley and Sons, which has taken several years of research.

Tools and the makers of tools have had a great part in creating the history of Sheffield.

The preserving and displaying of these tools is very important for future generations to be able to see and understand WHY and to some extent HOW these tools were made for use all over the world.

The telling of the story and history of the Barnsley family and firm in their specialised field is an extremely worthwhile piece of work and I am pleased to commend this book to you.

Ken Hawley M.B.E

The Hawley collection of tools is an internationally important collection of over 100,000 objects including edgetools, catalogues, measuring tools and oral history now housed at Sheffield's Kelham Island Industrial Museum where some of this vast collection is on display in the special Hawley Gallery.
See www.shef.ac.uk/hawley

Acknowledgements

I should like to acknowledge the help given by the staff in the Local Studies Library in Surrey Street whose response to one of my statements about 'this query being rather vague and unusual' commented that 'we do the vague and unusual' and promptly came up with the booklet I required.

We were also very glad of the help we received from a small band of people who saw the appeal for information that was placed in the *Sheffield Star* newspaper. They are acknowledged in the text. Special thanks to Eric Boocock who met me a couple of times one of which was in Cornish Street to walk around the outside of the works. Barbara Salvin spent time with me telling me stories about her parents, grandfather and great aunt, all of whom were Barnsley employees. Barbara is an administrator in a renovated building (Globe Works) that was once owned by the Barnsley firm and situated next to the now sadly derelict Cornish works.

Peter Machin a local historian was kind enough to lend to me a nineteenth century wages book of Barnsley's awl department.

Phil Ford, a family history researcher based in Sheffield, helped by looking for births, marriages and deaths that I could not find as well as seeking out land registry documents at Wakefield relating to the firm. Sadly Phil died very suddenly in May 2010. Property deeds used as sources of information in this book are a tribute to Phil's painstaking work.

Karen Lightowler (researcher of the Sheffield Flood 1864) is always generous with her time and has skilfully put together the family tree that appears in this book; she also gave other helpful advice.

Deborah Wheeldon helped with technical word processing details and made my cover design idea look more professional.

Responsibility for the text rests with me but this book could not have come into being without the enormous input of Colin Barnsley. He provided me with boxes full of old documents and photographs relating to the history of the family and the firm. This was the equivalent of buried treasure! He also helped me together with some of his staff, particularly Judith, to understand something of the tool making processes. His firm, Woodware Repetitions, in Mowbray Street Sheffield still produces many of the kinds of tools that were produced by George Barnsley and Sons. The Barnsley and Sons building still stands on the banks of the Don. Very important was Colin's boundless enthusiasm for the project. The discussions we had and the suggestions he made about directions to take ensured greater accuracy and thoroughness and helped to hone the book into a better quality publication than I could ever have achieved on my own.

There were at least five men who served in the armed forces in both wartime and peacetime. Two of them, George Barnsley (b.1874 son of Henry) and George Barnsley (b.1875 son of Joseph) were obviously descended through the male line. The other three were William Barnsley Allen a Barnsley descendent through his mother Edith Barnsley and Eugene Leclere through his grandmother Elizabeth Barnsley. Arthur Bentley whose father Tom Barnsley died when Arthur was about three years old has always been known by his stepfather's name. The information on Captain William Barnsley Allen is almost wholly from the website of Chris Hobbs and is used with his permission. His layout for his website has been kept with only minor adjustments to the pages in order to make them fit the printed page. My thanks to the families of two of the men, Nigel and Sue Allen and Leon and Mike Leclere (Eugene Leclere's son and grandson) for information and pictures.

Last but not least thank you to Pauline Jordan and Arthur Bentley for doing the essential task of proof reading the text and for suggestions of how to make the content more readable.

Contents

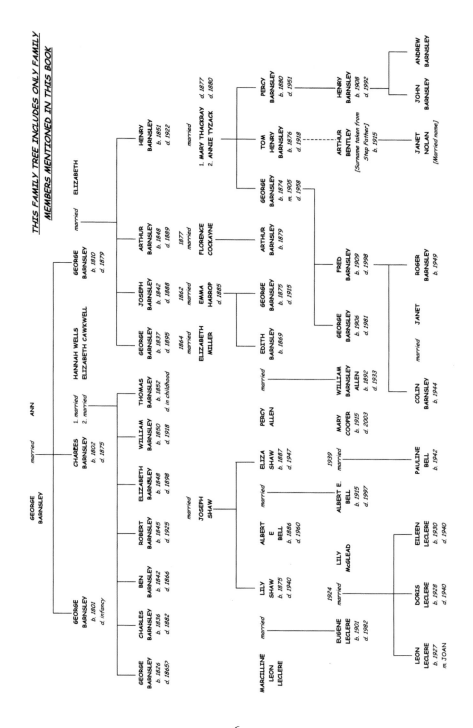

Part One
The Barnsleys of Sheffield pre 1800

Chapter 1

Missing links

When George Barnsley became Master Cutler in 1883 *The Sheffield Telegraph* (1) made reference to the fact that he was not the first George Barnsley to be made Master Cutler: another George Barnsley filled the role in 1650. It would have been good to establish some kind of family link between the two since both were cutlers but despite searching parish registers and historical records that has not yet proved possible.

The stumbling block is the fact that we have been unable to find any record of the marriage of the parents of George Barnsley born in 1810 who founded the firm. His baptism like that of his older brother Charles (also involved in the development of the firm) is recorded in the parish register of St. Peter's Sheffield. The parents are recorded as George and Ann Barnsley but their marriage was not recorded at St. Peter's. We know that George's mother Ann apprenticed him in 1824 to Thomas Wing, a file maker, and so by that year his father George must have been dead. Charles, who was about eight years older than George and a cutler, probably learnt his trade from his father whose occupation 'cutler' is shown in the baptism record for both Charles and George. The missing marriage record is crucial for us to know who this George's father was and what his trade was. The *International Genealogical Index* (IGI) has been searched, as have all parishes in South Yorkshire and North Derbyshire. In addition there is on record the baptism of a George Barnsley (same parents) and burial recorded a year or two before the birth of Charles. This puts the marriage around 1800.

Here are some possibilities. There is a George Barnsley who was baptised in March 1781 at St Peter's, son of George Barnsley and Hannah Barnsley (nee De Grave). The difficulties are that, if this George baptised in 1781 was the George who eventually married Ann, she was 10 years older than George (based on Ann's death certificate information). This George would therefore have been a minor at the time of the marriage. Moreover, if he were apprenticed then he would in theory have been unable to marry. He is only a possibility if his baptism was two or three years after his birth but that would have been unusual in that era. If she were a widow at the time of the marriage she could possibly have been older by 10 years or more. The George Barnsley who died in June 1817 aged 36 years would have had a birth date of 1781.

What seems conclusive to me, looking at the curation document appointing trustees for a George Barnsley minor, son of the George who died in 1817, is that this young man was left goods by his mother who is clearly cited as Hannah De Grave husband of George Barnsley deceased who in turn is described as a silversmith. One would expect that in a family of cutlers going back centuries, the son would follow his father's trade and we know from baptismal records that the George we are looking for (father of Charles and George) was a cutler rather than a silversmith.

There is another George Barnsley of Tenter Street who could be the one who married Ann but even if he is it does not help us get back to 1650. This George had a father Charles who would fit with the fact that George and Ann called their second-born child Charles. However Charles father of the George of Tenter Street was a poor child with a mother Frances Barnsley but no acknowledged father. There is her possible baptism in Sheffield parish registers for November 3rd 1725. Her father is George Barnsley but no occupation is given though a possible sibling for Frances (George baptised Jan 1st 1724) is recorded and the father George Barnsley is a cutler. Again we hit a brick wall, as there is no marriage recorded for a George Barnsley 1700-30 in the Sheffield register. We are therefore back in the position of having to make an assumption without proof that there is a link between the George Barnsley Master Cutler of 1650 and the one of the same name in 1883.

Notes

References for Part 1 of the book are listed at the end of the section on page 20.

In the sources used there are various spellings for Godderd Hill, e.g. Gotherd and Goddard. The policy has been to leave the spelling as in the source. The probability is that the Barnsleys lived in the only dwelling on that hill and that as they prospered it became Goddard Hall. A later building of that name once served as a nurses' home and still stands in the grounds of the Northern General Hospital.

Chapter 2

Earliest references to the Barnsley 'Clan'

We can only guess that some time several centuries ago a man walked from Barnsley to the Sheffield area and became known in his new community by his place of origin, perhaps George, John, William, Henry of Barnsley. Why he or possibly they came is lost in the mists of time. In the Sheffield area back in the Middle Ages there seems to have been Barnsleys to the east, the north and the west of the town. They may or may not have had a common ancestry though those in the northeast of Sheffield were very near what today would be Barnsley Road.

The earliest reference (2) I have been able to find is a John Barnsley who made a will in June 1548. His second wife Agnes proved the will on 20th April 1553. Sons named in the will are Sir George, Robert, Thomas, John, Nicholas and Henrie. Why was the eldest son *Sir* George? Apparently the lowest degree of knighthood was a knight bachelor and his role was to command a small unit of personal retainers. (3). Could this be the status of the Sir George named in this will? It is interesting that the feudal lord, George Talbot, the fourth Earl of Shrewsbury succeeded to the title in 1473 when aged 5. Did George become a local popular name in that period and is this the origin of the 'George' as in 'Barnsley'? It was a period when English history was turbulent at the time of Henry VII, the first of the Tudors. Later in the 16th century came the religious upheavals caused by the policies of Henry VIII, Edward, Mary 1 and Elizabeth. Whilst many remained Catholic, the official religion in the land varied depending on the monarch currently in power. Politically astute and careful, the Shrewsbury's seemed to remain fairly consistently Catholic and this was probably true of most of the folk who lived around the Sheffield Manor. However, in Sheffield there were other changes taking place.
George Talbot held high office from his king and lived in Sheffield in Manor Lodge. His guardian had started to build Manor Lodge to replace the old castle. Manor Lodge was far more substantial than a hunting lodge and George completed what his guardian had started. This George Talbot was frequently at court and wielded considerable power. He was also an experienced military leader. In 1513 he raised 4,437 men to go and fight in France though many of these would come from his other estates in Shrewsbury and Derbyshire. In the 1520s and later the Earls of Shrewsbury fought on the Scottish Borders in 1522,1532,1544-5,1548 and 1557.

In the mid 1500s *Hallamshire was a region of cattle and sheep rearing, sometimes with dairying on fells and moorland, and with corn and stock rising variously combined in clay vales. Sheffield was just a small market town: the bulk of the land was held by free burgage tenure, charged with a contribution to the yearly fee-farm payable to the earls. The inhabitants dealt with their lord as a community through their local bailiff. (4)* The Sheffield population at this time was about 2000 and included several hamlets. According to a paper in the Transactions of the Hunter Archaeological

Society (5) there was a depression in agriculture during the Middle Ages. This could have been a contributory factor in the development of cutlery making as an additional source of income for farmers.

The second son Francis succeeded George as the fifth Earl of Shrewsbury. Francis continued this political activity and maintained his position as President of the Council of the North under Henry VIII, Edward VI, Queen Jane, Mary 1and finally Elizabeth who, according to Mary Walton, disliked and feared him. Elizabeth did not dare during Francis' lifetime to impose her religious settlement on the unwilling North. Mary Walton judged Francis:

'as stopping short of the actively dishonourable, and whatever his private motives or policy, he acted as a brake on too violent a change and in the end probably did his country more useful service than many a better man. (6)

It seems that Francis was popular in the locality. Mary Walton describes local people as:

'an old fashioned race who liked a noble to live lavishly and behave like a prince. When the free tenants found themselves in trouble, through religious difficulties of the times, they turned naturally to him and he "stood good lord" to them'. (7)

There is at least a possibility that the Sir George in the John Barnsley will was a part of the retinue of the Earls of Shrewsbury. If this were the case it would explain why John Barnsley left the smythe (sic) to the three younger sons. Various items of clothing are distributed amongst the family including a leather dublett (sic) to John his heir as well as his 'carttes and wheilles'. (carts and wheels?). John his heir is distinguished from John the younger one of his named six children. John the younger got the 'doublett' as opposed to the leather 'doublett'. Of most interest is the fact that George was bequeathed a 'rockntre' which translated is a rocking-tree which was the axle from which the lay of a weaver's loom was suspended. (There were several weavers in the area at the time and this was in any case probably part of subsistence living in what was essentially a rural community) Three of John's children, Robert, Thomas and Nicholas, were to have the 'smythe' (smithy) so long as his wife lived and if they did not marry. It is difficult to know the purpose of these latter two clauses but the fact that John had a 'smythe' links the Barnsley name at a very early date to working with metal almost certainly in order to make tools. Only ten years later there is a reference found in the *Sheffield Manorial Records* for May 3rd 1568 to a George Barnsley.

'To the court came George Barnseley and took such mark to have use for himself as was aforesaid May 3rd 1568' The source of this quotation adds that 'the mark is not shown nor use stated.'(8) The Manorial Court was then the authority for granting makers' marks, what today we would call trademarks. Was this the same George (Sir George) named in the will of John above or perhaps a relative?

10

The earliest manorial roll to survive concerning the granting of marks is 1554. It contains the phrase 'if any other person should strike that mark and thereupon be convicted by verdict he should lose to the Lord xxs (20 Shillings) and make amendment to the injured party; and he gave to the lord id. of yearly rent.' (9) During the 16th century, Mary Walton suggests,

'Within a few years of the young George's succession to the Earldom, (1473) the little streams of Hallamshire, which so long had sung unheeded to the bilberries and hazel bushes rushed into history over the water-wheels of Sheffield. When this new opportunity offered, it was grasped so readily by the smiths of Hallamshire that it is plain they had already laid a foundation on which their successors could build a special skill'(10)

In 1624-25 in the list of cutlers, shearsmiths and scissorsmiths (11) already in the trade at the date of incorporation (Cutlers' Company) are George Barnsley, Robert Barnsley and Thomas Barnsley possibly the sons or grandsons of the men named in John Barnsley's will above. The cutlers had already been regulated for some time. The granting of marks could have been instituted in the time of Earl George or Francis but by 1578 some sixty marks had been registered. Mary Walton (p.50) records a typical set of regulations that has survived:

'The constitutions, ordainces and devises agreed ordeyned and maide' on 24th of June 1565, 'by the whole of the cutlers, makers of knyffes, and the cutler occupation whythin the lordshyppe of Halomeshire,' for 'mayntenance of the common welthe of cutler's craft and cutlers occupacion according to the aunncyante customes and ordainces by men of the said occupation there dwellinge, made and heretofore used', were drawn up with the consent of George, the sixth Earl of Shrewsbury, in the manor court. Two close seasons of a fortnight in August and a month at Christmas were instituted; the making of material supplied by outsiders, or the supplying of outsiders with partly finished articles, was forbidden; it was agreed that the period of apprenticeship should be seven years, and that only men so apprenticed could practice the craft. As the ordinances are expressly said to be in accordance with 'the ancient customs and ordinances,' the regulation of the trade certainly went back further than 1565 but no fragment of any earlier ordinances has survived.'

Two contemporary writers John Leland who travelled through England in 1536 to 1542 and Peter Bales who published a book in 1590 testify to the existence of a well-established trade in smything and cutlery in Hallamshire and Peter Bales recommended a Sheffield knife 'as best'. The sixth Earl also George had most of his energy taken up in guarding Mary, Queen of Scots, but it is interesting to note that when he was finally allowed to relinquish this duty he retired to Handsworth Hall, very close to where several Barnsleys lived. Apparently this George was very popular with his officers and tenants and always gave unremitting attention to local responsibilities. He died in 1590 by which time there were many ways in which Sheffield had become an urban community in that many of the tradesmen did not own land and were therefore not self-sufficient.

In 1621 the cutlers made moves to make better provision for the trade and in 1624 got the support of Sir John Savile, a knight of the Shire for Yorkshire. The Act was passed by Parliament in April of that year. This was the beginning of the Cutlers' Company whose hierarchy consisted of a Master, Wardens and Searchers. There were two Barnsleys in this latter group, George and Robert. In the records of the Cutlers' Company there are Barnsley names for several generations but their relationship one to the other is impossible to track.

In 1633 it is recorded that George Barnsley became free from the apprenticeship to his father also George Barnsley, cutler of Gotherd Hill. In 1670 a Joshua Barnsley whose father George Barnsley was deceased gained his freedom from another George Barnsley. Could this be the George Barnsley who had gained his freedom in 1633? George Barnsley of Gotherd Hill and of Crabtree (which is very much the same geographical area) is cited as master to apprentices starting to train in1638, 1655 and 1703. The date span would suggest these are different George Barnsleys, possibly sons or at least related because of the address.

The geographical location of Gotherd Hill and Crabtree would strongly suggest some family relationship between the various Barnsleys who appear as residents of Gothard Hill or Crabtree. (See map on page 13). In addition in the table beginning on page 16, which shows some apprenticeship records of the Cutlers' company in which Barnsleys are named there are also Barnsleys at nearby Piper House as well as at Longley. Peter Harvey (12) suggests that Piper Road, Piper Close and Piper Crescent in today's Sheffield 5 are named after a 17th century house called Piper House. The name probably came from one of the paid pipers or waits who combined the functions of town musicians with town watchman. They sometimes also called out the hours of the night. They were a recognised institution in many towns; for example in Manchester, Norwich, Bath and York as well as Sheffield where they were under the government of the Town Burgesses. The dates these Barnsleys had apprentices were 1670 (Joshua Barnsley gained his freedom), 1737 (John Barnsley gained his) and in 1780 (George Barnsley of Piper House took on another apprentice).

In these same records we also have Barnsleys whose address is given as Longley. This again is less than a mile from Gotherd Hill, Crabtree and Piper House suggesting yet another branch of the same family. Robert Barnsley took over property from Thomas Creswick of Burrowe lee (There is a Burrowlee Rd in Owlerton and Burrowlee House was built by Thomas Steade in 1711. His wife was Elizabeth Creswick).

'1621-2 March 2nd, in the 19th year of James 1st. Feoffment (Lat) whereby Thomas Creswicke of Burrowe lee in the parish of Ecclesfield in the county of York yeoman, in part perfoemane of a certain indenture made between him the said Thomas of the one part and Henry Shaw of le Hill in the* *chapelry of Bradfield in the said county, yeoman of the other part, gave, granted and enfeoffed and confirmed unto William Greene of Smallfield in the said county yeoman and Robert Barnsley of Longley in the said county cutler and their heirs; all and singular the messuages cottages out houses buildings gardens orchards crofts closes land meadows pastures feedings woods underwoods tenements and heriditaments of him Thomas, with all and singular the appurturtenances, situate lying and being in Ollerton and Wadsley in the said county of York; and the reversion and reversions remainders, of all and singular the said premises; to hold to the said William and Robert and the heirs of them and the longer liver of either of them, for ever.'(13)*

A feoffment is similar to a deed of gift, recording the sale of real property (land or buildings). It developed in the Middle Ages. In the above, Ollerton presumably means Owlerton.

William Fairbanks map of Sheffield Parish in 1795.The two lines in the bottom right hand corner point to Goddard Hill and Crabtree. H to right or eastside of map is about where Goddard Hall is today in grounds of Northern General Hospital.

13

Chapter 3

Harrison's Survey of the Manor of Sheffield 1637 and the Records of the Cutlers' Company

In this survey (16) there are over 20 entries under the name of Barnsley. These are almost certainly, some of the same men. The first names are George, Robert, Thomas, John and William. Robert had some land at Stumperlowe but either the same or a different Robert had land at Longley in the region of Shirecliffe Hall and a William Barnsley was a keeper at Rivelin. Of particular interest is the fact that George is named as having a part share in the Wheel at Wadsley. His rent was £1.11shillings a year. This wheel would seem to be what is now identified as Wadsley Forge and Wardsend Steelworks on the Don in the modern Wadsley Bridge area. It is known to have been in existence since at least 1581, the earliest known record when a George Hobson paid rent to the Shrewsbury estate 'for his new wheel at Wadsley Bridge'. In the 1637 survey George Barnesley, William Staniforth, Thomas Wilkinson, Richard Lee and John Rawson together had a half share of the Wadsley Wheel.

	£	s.	d.
	01	0	
William Beighton Ralph Purslove } for porter wheele	00		
William fforest	00		
George Smedley for a wheele in ye Whicker by Sembly Greene	08	10	
William Birley for A wheele in ye Whicker by Sembly Greene	08	10	00
Abraham Stockes for A wheele at Walke mill	08	00	00
Robert Carr and Humfrey Twigge for the forge wheele put In the Iron works Coll. Copleyes	18	00	00
Mr Bright for a wheele at Bright Side	05	00	00
William Hoole for A wheele at Bright Side	01	00	00
Gilbert Oates for a Wheele at Wadsley Bridge In Mr Copleys Iron Workes	04	10	00
William Wright John Parkin & } for halfe a Wheele at Wadsley	03	03	00
Ralph Smith	03	03	00
George Barnesley William Staniforth	1	11	0
Thomas Wilkinson - for ye other halfe of a Wheele at	00	15	10
Richard Lee & Wadsley	00	15	08
John Rawson	01	11	06
Godfrey Birley & William Hydes for halfe of Malin Bridge Wheele	02	04	00
Thomas Parkin	01	02	00
John Wild -for ye other halfe of Malin	00	11	00
William Matthewman Bridge Wheele	00	11	00
William Webster & Thomas Webster for a Wheele in Rivelin	02	08	0
Robert Skargill	00	06	0
Edward Webster & -for a Wheele in Rivelin	00	10	
Edward Greaves	00	10	
Robert Shimeild & for a Whele in Rivelin	01	10	
Thomas Spooner	00	10	
William Greaves & Edward Greaves for a Wheele in Rivelin	01		
Robert Shimeild for a parte of a Wheele in Rivelin	00		

£   s.   d.

Sum Totall 142—2—

There is no visible evidence of the wheel but the head-goit could still be seen south of Leppings Lane in 1989. Harrison also puts on record that the rivers of the Don, Sheaf, Loxley, Porter and Rivelin are profitable to the Lord in regard to the mills and cutler wheels which are turned by these streams 'which wheels are employed for the grinding of knives by four or five hundred Master workmen'. Harrison also comments on the availability of grinding stones hewn out in Rivelin.

In the same survey are many references to George Barnsley as the owner of land. (E.g., p.120 and 169)

847 Item a meadow called Penny Rent lying between the lands of George Barnsley North and William Bate South and abutteth upon the Lord's lands in the use of Hugh Beighton east and Willow Lane West.

464 Item a close of pasture and arable lying betweene the lands of George Barnsley in parte and pitts moore in parte East and the last piece North west.

All the information extracted from this survey indicates that the Barnsleys were at this stage in history a family of some substance who owned or leased land from the Lord of the Manor and were therefore doing some farming as well as being involved in the developing cutlery industry.

The history of the Cutlers' Company supports the view that the family were well known and of some substance. Leader states in his history of the Cutlers' Company that in 1564 there was a jury of cutlers (who were part of the manorial government system) who were responsible for granting marks. Amongst these jurors were the Rawsons, Barnsleys, Machons, Hills, Foxes Creswykes and others and this indicates 'the antiquity of families steadfastly associated with the hardware manufacture through many centuries'.

Early in the 17th century Leader points out that there were several wheels on the local rivers divided in various holdings, two or three tenants sometimes taking half a wheel and that their number represents capacity for a considerable output. He claims that there were the same number in 1604 as in 1637 when the Harrison survey was done but where the rent in 1637 was £3 it was only £1 in 1604. That indicates a steady rate of inflation. Leader also mentions that in 1624 'Adam Bate whose 1614 mark closely resembled Robert Barnsley's now chose a quaint sort of half moon face'.

Incorporation meant that the trade acquired a new dignity and men of all classes and trades sought to apprentice their sons. Apprenticeship was for 7 years and the apprentices often boarded with the Master. Leader reports that in 1647 George Barnsley junior of Gotherd Hill gave 16d a year towards his apprentice's apparel, although the boy's father Hugh Chalnor of Darnall had paid a premium of 40 shillings.

The company rules were never enforced very vigorously in terms of who was allowed in as a freeman and people bought their way in and informal arrangements continued for apprenticeships within a family. When the filesmiths were allowed in they were a constant source of friction in bending the rules.

Leader has another interesting paragraph concerning the Barnsley family. He writes: *Richard Jackson and George Barnsley, the latter a member of a family long resident at Gotherd (Goddard) Hill, and Thomas Bate, had like many of the predessors (sic) been in the Company from the beginning.* They had to wait long for promotion, and by this time 'the old gang' was extinct, a new generation having arisen to carry on the work. The Barnsley connection with the Mastership was revived in 1883 when another George Barnsley occupied the chair. Leader attributes to this George Barnsley 'the welcome innovation by which ladies, instead of being relegated as spectators to the gallery, grace the table with their company'. Since 1883 the practice of associating the Mistress Cutler as hostess with the Master Cutler as host, has been regularly followed.

Below is a table that I have constructed from the Cutlers' Company records (17) showing some Barnsley apprentices, parents and masters from 1627–1871. In the mid 1600s when a George Barnsley was Master Cutler the addresses given in these records indicate that all possible candidates are concentrated in the area of Goddderd or Gotherd Hill (now Goddard), Crabtree and Piper House.

APPRENTICE		PARENT			MASTER		
Name	Year	Name	Abode	Occupation	Name	Abode	Occupation
James BARNSLEY	1627	Robert BARNSLEY	Stumperlowe	Yeoman	Hugh HYDE	Walkley	Cutler
George BARNSLEY	1633(f)	George BARNSLEY	Goddderd hill	Cutler	George BARNSLEY	Goddderd Hill	Cutler
George BARNSLEY	1661	George BARNSLEY	Crabtree	Cutler	John HOWARD or HEWARD		Cutler
George BARNSLEY	1664	George BARNSLEY	Crabtree	Cutler	William TWIBELL		Cutler
Robert BARNSLEY	1667	George BARNSLEY	Crabtree hill	Cutler deceased	George senior MACHON	Pitsmoor	Scissorsmith
Robert BARNSLEY	1667?	George BARNSLEY	Crabtree hill	Cutler deceased	George junior MACHON		
Joshua BARNSLEY (f)	1670	George BARNSLEY	Goddderd hill	Deceased	George BARNSLEY		Cutler
William BARNSLEY	1670	William BARNSLEY	Fulwood	Husbandman	John FIRTH		Cutler
Jonathan BARNSLEY	1680	George BARNSLEY	Goddderd Hill	Yeoman deceased	JOSHUA	Longley	Cutler

APPRENTICE		PARENT			MASTER		
Name	Year	Name	Abode	Occupation	Name	Abode	Occupation
James BARNSLEY	1685	John BARNSLEY	Morayates		William Atkin	Lightwood	Scythesmith
Joseph BARNSLEY	1690	George BARNSLEY	Pitsmoor		George FOX		Cutler
Joshua BARNSLEY	1692	William BARNSLEY		Cutler	Samuel LEVICKE		Cutler
Joshua BARNSLEY	1692(f)	Joseph BARNSLEY	Longley	Cutler	Joseph BARNSLEY	Longley	Cutler
Joseph BARNSLEY	1698	George BARNSLEY	Crabtree	Cutler deceased	GEORGE		Cutler
John BARNSLEY	1699	Joshua BARNSLEY	Longley	Cutler deceased	Samuel STONES		Cutler
Jonathan BARNSLEY	1699	William BARNSLEY		Cutler	Joseph MICOCK		Cutler
George BARNSLEY	1699(f)	George BARNSLEY			George FOX		Cutler
Joseph BARNSLEY	1703	Joshua BARNSLEY	Longley	Cutler deceased	William SPEIGHT	Crabtree or Bridgehouses	Filesmith
Jonathan BARNSLEY	1707	Jonathan BARNSLEY		Cutler	William BIRKS		Cutler
Cornelius BARNSLEY	1708	Jonathan BARNSLEY		Cutler	Joseph SPEIGHT		Cutler
Ishbosheth BARNSLEY	1709	Jonathan BARNSLEY		Cutler	John TOPCLIFFE		
John BARNSLEY (f)	1719	George BARNSLEY	Piper House	Cutler			
Joshua BARNSLEY	1728	Jonathan BARNSLEY		Cutler deceased	Jeremiah BINGHAM		Cutler
Joseph BARNSLEY	1736	Jonathan BARNSLEY	Wicker	Cutler deceased	Joshua TWIGG	Attercliffe	Cutler
Thomas BARNSLEY	1736	Thomas BARNSLEY	Conisborough	Shoemaker	Lionel SMILTER		Cutler
John BARNSLEY (f)	1737	George BARNSLEY	Piper house	Cutler	George Barnsley	Piper House	Cutler
Jonathan BARNSLEY	1750(f)	Jonathan BARNSLEY		Cutler	Jonathan BARNSLEY		Cutler
Joseph BARNSLEY	1758	Edward BARNSLEY	Stoney Middleton	Labourer	Joseph SYKES		Filesmith
Charles BARNSLEY	1759	Francis BARNSLEY	Brightside		George WILSON		Cutler

17

APPRENTICE		PARENT			MASTER		
Name	Year	Name	Abode	Occupation	Name	Abode	Occupation
Samuel BARNSLEY	1762	Samuel BARNSLEY	Wicker	Weaver	Thomas UNWIN	Brightside	Scissorsmith
George BARNSLEY	1771(f)	Jasper BARNSLEY			Jaspar BARNSLEY		Cutler
George BARNSLEY	1772	Samuel BARNSLEY		Weaver	John WISE		Cutler
John BARNSLEY	1775	Jasper BARNSLEY		Cutler	Joseph WHITE		Cutler
George BARNSLEY	1780	Jaspar BARNSLEY		Cutler	Thomas PARRAMOUR		Cutler
John BARNSLEY	1783	George BARNSLEY	Bradwell	Husbandman	John junior SWIFT		Scissorsmith
John BARNSLEY	1783	Jasper BARNSLEY		Cutler	John SHEPHERD		
John BARNSLEY	1784	Joseph BARNSLEY	Eckington	Miller	Thomas GASKIN	Sheffield Park	Cutler
William BARNSLEY	1785	John BARNSLEY	Wolver-hampton	Whitesmith deceased	James PADLEY		Cutler
Jasper BARNSLEY (f)	1786	John BARNSLEY		Cutler	John Barnsley		Cutler
John BARNSLEY	1786	George BARNSLEY	Bradwell	Husbandman	Joseph HINCHCLIFFE		Scissorsmith
George BARNSLEY	1788	George BARNSLEY		Cutler	John JERVIS		Cutler
Joseph BARNSLEY	1792	Jonathan BARNSLEY		Cutler deceased	William WIGFALL		Knife maker
John BARNSLEY	1794	John BARNSLEY		Fork maker deceased	William WIGFALL		Knife maker
William BARNSLEY	1794	Jonathan BARNSLEY		Fork maker deceased	William WIGFALL		Knife maker
George BARNSLEY	1795	George BARNSLEY	Bridgehouses	Cutler deceased	George COOPER		Knife maker
George BARNSLEY	1796	George BARNSLEY		Plater deceased	William JESSOP		Knife maker
Thomas BARNSLEY	1796	Jonathan BARNSLEY		Fork maker deceased	William WIGFALL	Ecclesall Bierlow	Knife maker
John BARNSLEY	1797	Jonathan BARNSLEY		Fork maker deceased	Fraser NORTON		
Thomas BARNSLEY	1797	Jonathan BARNSLEY		Fork maker deceased	James VANCE		
William BARNSLEY	1797	Jonathan BARNSLEY		Fork maker deceased	Joseph DRABBLE		

APPRENTICE		PARENT			MASTER		
Name	Year	Name	Abode	Occupation	Name	Abode	Occupation
Joshua BARNSLEY	1798	Joseph BARNSLEY	Leeds	Clothier	Daniel CHAMPION		Scissorsmith
Joseph BARNSLEY	1800	George BARNSLEY	Bridgehouses	Knife maker deceased	Benjamin UNWIN		Filesmith
John BARNSLEY	1802	John BARNSLEY		Razor maker deceased	Daniel CORKER		Scissorsmith
Joseph BARNSLEY	1802	Joseph BARNSLEY		Silversmith	John WHITEHEAD		
Joseph BARNSLEY	1804	Joseph BARNSLEY		Silversmith	Joseph WHITTINGTON		Knife maker
John BARNSLEY	1813	George BARNSLEY		Razor grinder deceased	George HAYES		Knife grinder
George BARNSLEY	1871(f)				PURCHASE		Knife and filemaker

The above table also points up another possible family link in that it has at Bridgehouses a Barnsley family. George and Joseph Barnsley started apprenticeships in 1795 and 1800. The father who is deceased is described as cutler for George and knife maker for Joseph. In the family archives is a letter published in the 1930s in *The Sheffield Independent* about a house called 'The Towers' on Pye Bank which is in fact high up above what was the hamlet of Bridgehouses in the valley below. The writer of the letter claimed that the George Barnsley who founded the firm of George Barnsley and Co had lived in another house on Pye Bank near to The Towers. It seems George born 1810 did live there for a very short time. Pye Bank is his recorded address in White's directory (1852) though by 1856 he was living at Crookesmoorside according to the General Directory of Sheffield.

It is important to recognise that when knife making became a craft in the locality it was one of the ways in which small subsistence farmers supplemented their incomes. Without a doubt they worked near to their own homes and eventually rented time on one of the many water wheels on one of the Sheffield rivers. From the will of John Barnsley (1548) we see that he had a smithy and must therefore have made tools. From Manorial records and Cutler's Company records Barnsleys were deeply involved in the development of the cutlery trade both as practitioners, trainers of the next generation and in forming and running the more formal organisation of the trade as expressed in the organisation of the Cutlers' Company. They were a prominent family in their community. This continued through the 19th and 20th centuries in the family of George Barnsley and Sons, tool manufacturers and continues today with Woodware Repetitions who own the registered name of George Barnsley and Sons and is the firm sitting on the other bank of the Don just a little way down river and run by Colin, Janet and Roger Barnsley.

References in all of Part 1

(1) *Sheffield Daily Telegraph*, Friday September 7th 1883
(2) Walker Hall T. 'Sheffield 1287-1554. *A catalogue of Ancient Charters* Sheffield Local Studies Reference 016.942745
(3) Hey, David, (1996) *The Oxford Companion to Local History and Family History*. p.256, OUP
(4) Quoted in Bernard G.W. *The Power of the Early Tudor Nobility*
(5) 'A book of feudal aids made by the Earl of Shrewsbury in 1451' in *Transactions of the Hunter Archaeological Society Vol. 1 1914-18* pp-`39-140
(6) Walton, Mary (1948) *Sheffield and its achievements*, p.47
(7) Ibid p.38
(8) Walker Hall T. compiled and annotated by, (1928) *A descriptive catalogue of Sheffield Manorial Records* etc Sheffield Local Studies Ref. 016.94277SST
(9) Walton, Mary, Op cit p.38.
(10) Ibid p.49
(11) http://freepages.history.rootsweb.com/~exy1/text/cutlers_1624-1630.txt
(12) Harvey, Peter (1991) *Street Names of Sheffield,* Sheaf Publishing
(13) . Walker Hall T translated by, Wheat Collection Catalogue. Sheffield Local Studies Library 016.94274
(14) Walton, Mary Op cit p.142-143
(15) Flavell N. (2009) *Rotative Steam Engines in Sheffield before 1820, South Yorkshire Industrial Society Journal No.4 2007 (2009)*
(16) *Harrison's Survey of Sheffield Manor 1637* p.131
(17) See http://www.sheffieldrecordsonline.org.uk/data/search_app.php as well as:
Leader R.E.-(1905) *History of the Company of Cutlers in Hallamshire Vol 1* Pawson and Brailsford Sheffield

Part 2
George Barnsley and Sons

Chapter 1

The Barnsleys of Sheffield

Between 2003 and 2007 I went several times into Cornish Street to visit or take pictures of what was originally the James Dixon silversmith works. By this date their building had been renovated and converted into luxury apartments. The building on the other side of Cornish Street always saddened me as it was in such a state of disrepair and with all kinds of vegetation growing out of the windows and roof.

Photograph taken October 2006 in Cornish Street looking towards Green Lane and the town centre.

It had been the works of George Barnsley and Sons who had been as far as I knew at the time toolmakers. My father had always said that we were related to the Barnsleys and that his great uncle had been the Master Cutler. I was never very sure about this. Later research has shown that he was almost right in that his grandmother *Elizabeth Barnsley* was first cousin to the George Barnsley who was Master Cutler in 1883. My father was in fact his first cousin twice removed!

In addition he also claimed that there had been some kind of family disagreement and that our side of the family had completely lost out. He could only have heard this from his mother Eliza Shaw as both my father's grandparents on her side of the family had died by the time she got married. Judging by where the two sides of the family, (his grandmother being *Elizabeth Barnsley*), lived in Sheffield and their occupations within the firm during the 1850s onwards I would guess that this disagreement if it did happen was between the brothers *Charles* born 1802 and George born 1810. (There had been another sibling also called George who was born in February 1801 and who died in infancy). George born 1810 appears to have been the founder of the firm even though *Charles* according to land registry documents did put some money into the first buildings bought in Cornish Street. It could be that the brothers whose father is described in both their baptism records as a cutler started the firm together by renting at previous premises (see next section). *Charles* as a cutler and George as a filemaker had very differing skills to bring to a tool making venture.

The story then is the tale of two families: George whose descendents were to be the owners of the firm for many generations and *Charles* (my ancestor), George's older brother. A deed in the Land Registry at Wakefield reveals that George and *Charles* together bought the original part of Cornish works in Cornish Street in January 1851. Both families had offspring of the same name and the brothers George and *Charles* had wives of the same name, Elizabeth, though *Charles's Elizabeth* was his second wife. **To try to differentiate between the family members of the two brothers I have used italics to indicate members of *Charles's* family.**

It seems that *Charles's* involvement at managerial or ownership level lasted only until June 1854 as there is a supplementary deed whereby the land was registered under the names of George Barnsley and Philip Hepenstall. It seems that the latter was a valuer and agent to the Leeds and West Riding Protection Society and so it appears that the property may have been mortgaged. Perhaps *Charles* was not willing to take the risk or perhaps George wanted to go it alone and bought *Charles* out. Was this the point at which they had a disagreement or was it an amicable settlement?

We know for certain that the father *Charles* (a blade hardener) as well as his younger sons, *Ben* (a file forger), *William* (a file hardener) and *Robert* (a file forger) were working in 1864 as employees of George Barnsley and Sons as their names are recorded as Barnsley employees in the claims 'for loss of a week's wages' following the Sheffield Flood. *Ben* and *Robert* received one pound, *Charles* one pound and five shillings, *William* one pound and ten shillings. It is interesting that these three followed the trade of their Uncle George rather than that of their father *Charles.*

We know from census returns in 1841 and 1851 that both *Charles's family* and George's family lived in Allen Street or Upper Allen Street, which was the opposite side of Shalesmoor from Cornish Street.

To get to the Cornish Works when the firm moved there in 1851 would have meant crossing Shalesmoor. Wheeldon Street where the firm was in the 1840s was even closer, being off Solly Street which ran parallel to Allen Street. Cornhill where they were in 1849 was also in the same small area of

Sheffield. They were less than a mile from any of the three addresses occupied by the firm at different times in its development.

Picture taken in Allen Street in 1930s some
60 years after the Barnsley families lived there.
www.picturesheffield.co.uk

By 1851 George appears on the census as a file manufacturer and steel refiner employing 43 men and *Charles* as an assistant warehouseman though the entry is difficult to read. *Charles* lived at 179 Upper Allen Street and George his brother at 204. *Charles* eldest son *George* left Sheffield and went to work as a machine builder in an iron works in Chadderton, Lancashire. Chadderton is now in Greater Manchester. He moved there between the 1851 census and the 1861 census. It is definitely his name on the census return as the names of his wife and children are the same and the ages fit. In addition *Charles* the half brother next to him in age was living with *George's* family in Chadderton and missing from the Sheffield census. In 1861 *George* was about 35 years old and *Charles* about 23 and his occupation was cited as being the same as that of his older half brother, machine maker at iron works. In Sheffield on the previous census this same *George* was a spring knife cutler.

What made them go? *George* may have felt he had no prospects or was he leaving the situation because of some grievance. On the other hand he was the only child of *Charles's* first marriage to *Hannah* and was only 10 years younger than his stepmother. It is all conjecture but I wonder if this departure is linked in some way to family disagreements within the firm, or perhaps *George* didn't get on with his stepmother *Elizabeth*. I feel this is a less likely reason simply because by the time he left Sheffield he was married with a family of his own. Young *Charles* eventually left Manchester and returned to Sheffield. On the 1871 census he is back at his parents' home and described on the census as a scissor grinder. As far as I know George Barnsley and Sons did not make scissors so it may be that *Charles* chose not to work for them on his return or there was simply no vacancy.

By 1861 George has moved house to Spring Hill Road off Crookesmoor Road. I am sure this was a better residential area than Upper Allen Street where *Charles* continued to live. *Charles* is now recorded as a shoe blade hardener. It was for the making of tools for shoemakers and leather workers for which the George Barnsley firm became world-renowned. George is simply recorded as a file manufacturer and William a younger son as a file cutter. The eldest son also George who was to become the Master Cutler was already married and was living in Montgomery Place which I think from the entry in the 1862 White's trade directory was off St Philip's Rd. He is described as a commercial traveller, is married to Elizabeth and they have a servant Anne Lunn. Two of *Charles's* sons still living at home are *Ben* a file forger and *Robert* a file cutter. *Charles's* daughter *Margaret* aged 15 is a warehouse girl.

By 1871 George is an employer of 130 workers and is living in Oxford Street. He has also served on the council for a few years as the representative of St Philip's Ward, the ward in which the Cornish Works was situated. As far as I can tell, the only committee to which he belonged was the Highway Committee. In 1867 it seems that 460 yards of three-coat asphalting had been put on footpaths in Sheffield. This included those in Cornish Street and on Waterloo Footpath.

Most of George's sons still connected with the firm including George the future Master Cutler, and Joseph were by this time living in Oxford Street. Arthur had moved there by 1881 though George the elder and founder of the firm had died by that date. William his son died before reaching adulthood. William's twin Joseph died aged 46 in 1888 and Arthur in Chapel en le Frith in1889 aged 41. In the 1880s Oxford Street would have been in a smart area (just behind where Sheffield University is now). By 1891 Arthur's widow, Florence, was living on her own means still in Oxford Street and their son, George's grandson also Arthur, was at boarding school in Loughborough. He is missing from the family on the Sheffield census but a boy named Arthur Barnsley of the same age and born in Sheffield is recorded on the Loughborough census as one of many boys in this boarding school. In contrast *Charles's* grandchildren who moved with their parents to Chadderton were at the same age as Arthur working in the Lancashire cotton mills. *Charles* never moved and those of his sons who survived and lived in Sheffield were still in the area around Allen Street. His widow *Elizabeth* earned her living as a midwife.

In the context of the times it is obvious that by the 1870s George's side of the family can be numbered amongst the affluent merchant or middle class whereas *Charles's* family remained artisans. When George the file maker who founded the firm died in 1874, his will indicates that this is a 'rags to riches' story. This is a summary of its contents:

All household goods such as furniture, plate, linens, fuel, consumable provisions etc were left to his wife Elizabeth Barnsley.

To each of his daughters: Elizabeth, the wife of Henry Harrap and Annie the wife of Walter Carr, the legacy of £200 to be paid 'immediately after my decease'.

To the treasurer of the Boys Charity School £30.

To grandson, George Alfred Edman. Son of late daughter Charlotte, wife of Fredrick Woolfit Edman £1200 to be invested and payable to him at age 21. If he dies before that it reverts to GB's four sons and two daughters in equal amounts.

To brother *Charles Barnsley* £5 and a suit of mourning, to nephew *Robert Barnsley* £2 and a suit of mourning

To William Bolloroz?, George Keyworth?, Thomas Clarke, James Short?, 'workman(sic) in the employ of my firm' £2 each and a suit of mourning.

To his wife for her lifetime the house in Oxford Street where they currently reside to be kept in good repair etc. When she dies it goes in equal shares to the 4 sons.
His wife to receive an annuity from the profits of the firm of £156 per annum paid in weekly payments of £3 'on Saturday in every week clear of all deductions'.

The freehold, workshops, buildings, appliances and processes to be held in common by his four sons, George, Henry, Joseph, Arthur as tenants in common and their heirs.

To his daughters Elizabeth Harrap and Annie Carr a further £1000.

There is some complex provision made for Elizabeth Harrap I think relating to the use of the £1000 for her children in the event of her death. All the women are given control of their money independent of husbands or future husbands.

His total effects were under £14000. Modern equivalent £1,018,650 (one million, eighteen thousand six hundred and fifty pounds using Bank of England calculator).

The trustees (executors) were the four sons and Fredrick Woolfit Edman (Charlotte, his daughter's widowed husband).

What remains clear is that in very different capacities, members of both families at least for a couple of generations, were part of the Barnsley family firm. It is possible that Joseph Shaw who married my great grandmother *Elizabeth Barnsley,* a daughter of *Charles* was an employee. If he was, was their son *James Shaw* my great uncle also an employee of the firm? It seems very possible, as *Joseph* was a file hardener in 1881 and *James* also in 1891. They also lived in Douglas Rd and that is where *Charles's* son *Robert Barnsley* lived in 1881 and he was a file forger. We know from flood records that *Robert* worked for the firm.

By the time we reach my generation such differences have disappeared. Amongst *Charles's* grandchildren, one became an accountant and one of his sons had a multi-million pound business listed on the stock exchange. Another grandson had a distinguished career in the Royal Navy serving in WW2 and his son became a bank manager. My father was an engineer and then set up a very successful fruit and florist business which his son, my brother, continued to run until defeated by the supermarkets when he switched to property development. I became a teacher and later a training and development consultant. Of George's descendants several generations continued to run the family firm until it closed at the end of 2003, though one of George's descendants left the firm in the 1970s and together with his son took over a business, Woodware Repetitions on the opposite side of town. Later they moved to Mowbray Street on the opposite side of the Don less than a mile from where the family firm was situated in Cornish Street. Later another of George's great grandsons joined Woodware Repititions. Under this name the same kind of quality tools are made for the leather trade as George Barnsley and Sons made for many generations. Woodware Repititions have now registered the name of George Barnsley and Sons so that they can use it for trading purposes.

Chapter 2

The beginnings of the firm

The business was launched in 1836 just one year before Queen Victoria came to the throne. It is generally accepted that the founder was George Barnsley who began making and selling files in Wheeldon Street in the Brookhill area possibly working with his brother Charles, a cutler. According to the baptism records of what is now Sheffield Cathedral his father also George was a cutler. Metalwork was therefore in the blood. In addition Sheffield had for many centuries had a reputation as a centre for working metal. The geographical location was an important factor in all of this, the many rivers providing waterpower in the early days. Other natural resources were in or near to the region providing grinding stones, iron ore and eventually coal. Cutlery was in Sheffield dialect 'anything what cuts'. It included knives as well as implements like sickles and scythes. Other products were either flatware, for example forks and spoons, or holloware, which is any item made to contain something else, such as a jug for ale. It follows therefore that the resources and skills required for file making and for making cutting tools were already present in the local area. The production of files and cutting tools was to be a hugely significant development for George Barnsley and Sons.

In Geoffrey Tweedale's book *Steel City* (1) he cites the firm as an example of Sheffield's success in niche marketing. Many firms came to specialise in tools for specific work contexts. Burgon and Ball made hand-operated sheep shears as did Ball Bros. Dyson's at the Abbeydale Works made agricultural scythes, hay knives and grass hooks. George Barnsley and Sons became the leading manufacturer of tools for shoemakers and leather workers. When Colin Barnsley introduced me to the 'Dictionary of Leather Working Tools'(2) I noticed that there were only two Sheffield firms other than Barnsley's cited in the list of manufacturers. One was Thomas Wing and the other was James Oxley. The latter was taken over by Barnsley's in 1968.

George and James Oxley were in Garden Street, Sheffield. I found a couple of early documents in Sheffield Archives. The one on the next page is a 'printers' proof' for a catalogue of some kind. The first section lists types of shoe knives.

27

PRICES OF
KNIVES, STEELS, &c.
MANUFACTURED BY
G. & J. OXLEY,
36 Garden Street, SHEFFIELD.

SHOE KNIVES.

	No. 020	021	022	023	024	025	027	028
Common Steel, square and round points	4	4¼	4½	5	5¼	5½	6	6½ inches.
	1s3½d	1s4d	1s6d	1s7d	1s10d	2s1d	2s7d	3s2d per doz.
Shear Steel, common glazed	No. 20	21	22	23	24	25	27	28
	1s6d	1s8d	1s7d	1s9d	2s0d	2s4d	2s10d	3s6d per doz.
Ditto ditto best ditto	No. 1	3/	3 2	33	34	36	3/	33
	1s6d	1s7d	1s8d	1s10d	2s1d	2s6d	2s11d	3s7d per doz.
Ditto ditto warranted ditto	No.							
	1s7d	1s8d	1s8d	1s11d	2s2d	2s8d	3s0d	3s8d per doz.
Ditto ditto Scale tangs, pinned ditto	No. 21½							
	2s1d	2s5d	2s6d	2s6d	2s8d	2s11d	3s5d	4s0d per doz.

Shear Steel, ladies' best glazed, stained handles, brass ferrules, No. 127, 1s10d | Through tangs, 6d. doz. extra | Stained handles, 6d. per doz. extra
Ditto ditto ditto warranted ditto ditto ditto 12s, 1s11d | Pin through the tang, 3d. do. | Ditto, with brass loops, 3s. do.
Ditto do. Leather cutting-out knives, No. 40, 5in. 6s | Best knives, No. 44, 3s4d | Improved best knives, No. 47, 4s6d
Newly invented double edged side peg knives, 13s. per dozen. | Peg rasps, 15s. per dozen.

BREAD KNIVES.

	No. 89	90	92	93	94	95	96	97
Shear Steel, Red handles	4½	5	6	6½	7	8	—	9 inches.
Brass ferrules	2s4d	2s3d	2s7d	2s9d	3s6d	4s8d	5s9d	7s2d per doz.

Bread, and Butter knives, of first quality and style, in cocoa, rosewood, &c.

BUTCHERS' AND COOKS' KNIVES.

	No. 050	051	052	054	055	056	057	058	059	450	451
Shear Steel, diamond beech handles	4½	5	5½	6	6½	7	8	9	10	11	12 inch.
	2s1d	2s6d	2s11d	3s5d	4s0d	4s7d	5s1d	7s9d	9s0d	11s8d	14s0d dz.
Ditto, cocoa, box, barwood, and yew do.	3s6d	3s6d	3s8d	4s3d	4s10d	5s6d	6s9d	8s8d	10s4d	13s0d	15s9d ,,
Ditto, partridge and rosewood ditto	3s4d	3s5d	3s10d	4s6d	5s0d	5s9d	7s0d	9s0d	10s9d	13s6d	16s3d ,,
Best ditto, beech flat handles	No. 60	61	63	64	65	70	71	72	73	74	75 inch.
	3s0d	3s3d	3s9d	4s4d	5s0d	5s8d	7s6d	9s0d	11s6d	14s6d	17s6d dz.
Do. do. partridge & rosewood, brass pins	4s2d	4s5d	5s0d	5s7d	6s4d	7s0d	8s6d	10s8d	13s6d	16s6d	19s6d ,,
Do. do. Dudley butchers' knives, do.	6s9d	7s0d	7s9d	8s6d	9s6d	10s6d	13s6d	16s0d	20s0d	24s0d	28s0d ,,

Brass saw screws, 3d. per screw extra.
Handled in box, cocoa, ebony, buck, stag, &c. in great variety.

TABLE STEELS. | BUTCHERS' STEELS.

No.		doz.			doz.	No.		doz.
201 Stag handle, full sized blade		5s0d	1 Black japanned handles		4s10d	2 Pressed tip		6s
202 Tip do. do.		5s6d	3 Self tip or horn		7s11d	151 Good stag, dog swivel		7s
140d Stag, polished and fluted do.		15s0d	228 Solid do. London pattern		16s0d	152 Best do. buck bolster		4s

Table and butchers' steels, in great variety, from 4s. to 40s. per doz.

PALLETTES.

	No. 130	131	132	133	134	135	136	137	138	139
Plain bolsters, Cocoa handles	3	4	5	6	7	8	9	10	11	12 inches.
	3s4d	3s7d	4s8d	8s0d	8s0d	10s6d	13s9d	17s4d	22s0d	29s0d per doz.
Do. ballanced	No. 140	141	142	143	144	145	146	147	148	149
	4s4d	4s8d	5s4d	7s0d	9s6d	11s10d	15s0d	19s6d	24s0d	31s0d per doz.

PAINTERS', PLUMBERS', AND GLAZIERS' KNIVES.

No.					3½	4	4½	5½ in.
305 Stopping knives, elastic, 3½ in. 5s6d; 4½ in. 5s8d doz.				Hack knives, thick backs,	5s4d	5s8d	6s0d	6s8d dz.
561 Putty knives, 4 in. spear and square points, 4s7d ,,				leather handles			5s11d	
505 Ditto ditto knotched, 3½ in. 5s6d; 4½ in. 6s6d ,,				Plumbers' shave hooks, 8s6d and 10s per doz.				

Basket makers' picking knives, 4s. 6d. per dozen. | Farriers' knives, from 8s. per dozen.
Ditto ditto hand knives, 5s. and 5s. 6d. ,, | Oyster ditto from 5s. ,,
Ditto ditto bodkins, from 5s. per dozen. | Gilders' knives, &c.

[B] URTON, PRINTER, SHEFFIELD.

We know that George who founded the firm of George Barnsley and Sons started his apprenticeship with a Thomas Wing in 1823. I have found only one possible Thomas Wing who was both a file maker and was of the right age to have an apprentice. He was based in Rockingham Lane in 1834 according to the Pigot Directory. Wing's son John also a file maker had a business on Gloucester Place, Spring Lane. However John had only one daughter Ann who married a John Burnell and they inherited John Wing's estate. The last company that John was involved with was that of his brother Charles (John Fern and Co) and that was situated in Allen Street which is where George Barnsley lived around the time he started the business. (See 1841census). One of Ann Wing's descendants, John Slingsby, tells me that both the Wings had 'file manufacturer' on their marriage records and that this is confirmed in Trade Directories. The Wings died out in 1886 when John Wing died. John had sold his business as a file and steel manufacturer in 1869. My theory is that George Barnsley's eventual 'niche market' in tools for leather workers was in some way influenced by his work with Thomas Wing. It seems at least possible that he took the idea and maybe even some of the customers from Thomas Wing when Thomas ceased working.

There is definite evidence that he was an apprentice to Thomas Wing a file maker and that the indenture was signed on June 4th 1823(3). Since it was his mother Ann who arranged this we can be very sure that his father was dead. There is the death of a George Barnsley recorded in the burial records of St Peter's Church Sheffield on July 4th 1816. He was a cutler and aged 47 with a last abode of Tenter Street. If his father had not died the young George would more than likely have learnt the cutlery trade from his father. It is probable that *Charles* born eight years earlier learnt his trade mostly from their father as he appears on the 1841 census return as a spring knife cutler. In 1851 he is working in a warehouse probably in the family firm. In 1861 he is a shoe blade hardener. By 1865 we know with certainty from the flood records that he worked for George Barnsley and Sons.

Charles's warehouse employment in 1851 seems a bit odd unless it was a job that was seen more as 'management' in today's language. Why had he returned to his original trade as an artisan by the time of the 1861census where he is described as a shoe blade hardener? Everything is conjecture. He may have been inefficient in the warehouse. On the other hand he may have simply disliked it and have felt more comfortable using the skills for which he had been trained. It interests me that in 1851, *Charles's* eldest son *George* was a spring knife cutler. He probably learnt his trade from his father. It was during the next decade (1851-1861) that he moved to Chadderton and became a machine maker in an iron works. It seems certain that if there was a rift it occurred between 1851 and 1861. It is worth noting that as time progressed it was for the cutting tools as well as for files that the firm established its formidable reputation.

Chapter 3

Father and Sons

George Barnsley, the father, (1810-1879) set up the business in 1836 probably with the involvement of his brother *Charles* as his name appears on the land registry documents for the purchase of the building that was the beginnings of the Cornish Street works, though he quickly fades from the picture as an owner. George's eldest son also called George was born a year later in 1837. This bust of George senior was displayed in the works and is now in the possession of one of his descendents, though there are three altogether, one of which was donated to the Cutlers' Company.

George Barnsley (1810-1879) founder of the firm.

A likeness of his son is a line drawing that appeared on September 29th 1883 in a supplement about the cutlers' feast in Martineau & Smith's Hardware Trade Journal (4). One of his descendents has the photograph from which this likeness was reproduced. According to the same source there was a portrait painted of him by Mr H.F.Crighton and presented to him by his work people at the beginning of his year as Master Cutler. The whereabouts of this are not known but in his will he bequeathed it to Henry his only surviving brother, he himself having no children.

The father is credited in this same source as having been a man of great determination, shrewdness and energy. He was his own traveller and found purchasers for his files in different places. In 1841 he is missing from the census return though his wife Elizabeth and the children are recorded as being in Allen Street. So far I have not found him on the 1841 census night anywhere in England. He could even then have been abroad. It is said that he was committed to the belief that 'success was dependent on quality'.

I think that it was the willingness to travel to find his own markets that may have been at least part of the reason for his success in building the firm to such a substantial size. I found a research paper (5) in Sheffield Local Studies Library describing the very common practice of Sheffield craftsmen to work more or less alone in their own homes or in workshops near their homes sometimes 'trading skills' with others in the process of producing, for example, a knife. However it seems that most such workers then depended on 'factors' or middlemen to find them markets for their goods. There was also a tendency to work only the hours necessary to earn a living. If George in the early days could produce enough to 'stockpile' products and then go out and find his own markets he would have an immediate advantage.

George the son joins the firm

George Barnsley (1837-1895) Master Cutler 1883

George the son was 13 when he joined his father in the firm and a year later he became his father's traveller. He must have had a real talent for selling as well as lots of drive and energy as he opened up new markets in London, Scotland, Ireland and other parts of England. When he was 21 his father made him a partner in the firm and the firm became George Barnsley and Sons. Eventually all the sons were to join the business, Joseph, Arthur and Henry. According to the Sheffield Daily Telegraph (10th Sept 1883), two of them had charge of the home travelling and the other two of the Continental. George was away from home in 1881 when the census was made. Later in life his business success was to make him a significant figure both as Master Cutler and in local politics. (See later chapter). He is described as a typical Yorkshireman 'hearty, genial and straightforward with remarkable determination. Physically he is large and full of energy - set on broad massive shoulders is a grand square head bespeaking capacity for work and brains to think it out to the best advantage' (6).

It appears that the firm was fairly early in achieving mechanisation particularly in filemaking. In the 1860's there was discussion in the industry about achieving the same quality of file by the use of machines than could be achieved by hand. It was claimed that this had been done in America and that such a machine was also doing it in Manchester. Sheffield workmen were opposed to this. The reasons given were that the skilled workman adapted the strength of his blow to the kind of steel being worked and even adjusted the fall of his chisel to keep the indentations even as he felt varying degrees of softness within the same blank. The skill in achieving this precision was so great that to our eye in the second millennium it would look as though it had been made by machine. An article in The Sheffield Telegraph on August 5th 1886 reports that *'The relative merits of files cut by machinery have been for some years the subject of dispute: but during the last year or two the advocates of machine cutting have grown more confident, and hence the controversy has waxed still keener. It is a matter of fact that machines have, during recent years, been brought more extensively into use no doubt for reasons of economy in production, and whereas three or four years ago only a small proportion of local manufacturers employed mechanical means, at the present time probably the majority of them use machines to a greater or lesser extent.*

The writer of the supplement on the 1883 Cutlers' Feast comments on his visit to the works of George Barnsley and Son that the '*many and ingenious machines for doing automatically what had long been considered as impossible except by hand labour were a sight to watch'*. It seems that under George's management the firm was embracing modern technology as it appeared. In his speech as the new Master Cutler at the Cutlers Feast in 1883 George said that there was a need *'to adapt ourselves in our manufactures to the requirements of the world. We have the consumption of our manufactures increased year by year, and I venture to give it as my opinion, that with the innate talent of our workmen and the introduction of machinery where it is practicable, we shall remain head and shoulders above every town in the world in our staple trades, and we shall keep up our ancient prestige'* (7). Sheffield probably did achieve this up to the 1930s when the world wide economic depression followed by WW2 led to the rise of competition from the Far East, particularly Japan, and later India.

It seems however that he also respected the past. Apparently at the Cornish Works he kept what is described as a 'sentry-like box', which fifty years previously had served as his father's warehouse. It contained the modest selection of files that he had previously kept at home to sell to the customers of the day.

The Sheffield Telegraph on September 10th 1883 reported the occasion when George Barnsley, having just become Master Cutler, gave a feast at the Cutlers' Hall for 400 of the workpeople and their spouses. This was the occasion when they presented him with an oil painting of himself *'as a token of their respect and esteem for him'*.

As Master Cutler in 1883 George gave appropriate leadership on behalf of Sheffield's cutlery firms. I quote (8):
Of particular annoyance to the company was the observation that whereas British Legislation provided remedies in cases where British residents fraudulently applied foreign names of cities on products no such legislation appeared to exist in France and Germany. A deputation from the company consisting of the Master Cutler, George Barnsley, one of the searchers J.F. Atkinson and the Law clerk, Herbert Hughes attended the Foreign Office in April 1884 and urged that efforts be made to ask the German Government to enact laws which would prevent goods being marketed with misleading indications of origin. However both the Foreign Office and the Board of Trade were unwilling to press the German government to alter its legislation. (Board of Trade to Foreign Office, No2, No4).

The same source indicates that a way forward was opened up by the Paris Convention for the Protection of Industrial Property 1883 to which Britain acceded in 1884. This was a union for the protection of industrial property (patents, industrial designs and trade marks). Other countries were slow to implement it and in fact Germany did not do so until after WW1.

George also served on the local council and represented St. Philips' Ward. In 1884 and 1885 he was on the Watch Committee which was responsible for law and order, street lighting and markets.

The three other brothers, Joseph (1842-1888), Henry (1847-1922) and Arthur (1851-1889) also went into the business. Joseph was apparently educated in France and Germany in order to be involved with the firm's links to European countries.

These included not only France and Germany but also Austria and Hungary. The firm also had business interests in Australia and other parts of the then British Empire including Africa. The brothers had equal shares in the company. This is probably why Arthur's widow was of independent means according to the 1891 census return. George himself had no children. Two of the brothers died at a relatively young age: Joseph was about 46 and Arthur

38. By 1891 Henry was a widower. I cannot find him or any of his family on the 1891 census so he may have been abroad with the children. In 1901 he is still in the business, as are at least two of his sons, George and his half brother Percy, the two still living at home. On the census return they have staying with them a visitor, Mabel Gittus, who came from Suffolk and who married George in 1905. Tom the other son does not appear ever to have been involved in the business but became an entertainer.

Henry Barnsley (1847-1922) left and Joseph (1842-1888)
The picture is described as having been taken with a customer.
Joseph is on the right.

References

(1) Tweedale Geoffrey, 1995.*Steel City, (Entrepreneurship, Strategy and technology in Sheffield 1743-1993)* p.162.Clarendon Press
(2)   Salaman R.A1986. *Dictionary of Leather-Working Tools c. 1700-1950 and the tools of allied trades pxiii.* George Allen and Unwin
(3) George Barnsley apprenticeship indenture to Thomas Wing of Sheffield, filemaker 4 June 1823. *Sheffield Archives.*
(4) Illustrated in *Supplement to Martineau and Smith's Hardware Trade Journal September 29th 1883*   .
(5) Hill, *An account of some trade combinations in Sheffield 1830's – 1850's*
(6) Op. cit. Martineau page 17.
(7) Ibid.
(8) Binfield Clive and Hey David 1997(eds). Pp.93-94 Oxford University Press

Chapter 4

George Barnsley and Sons, toolmakers

The manufacture of files was very important for the firm at the outset. It seems more than likely that George began in Wheeldon Street in the time-honoured way as a 'little mester' probably working on his own. Many such workers used other 'little mesters' in part of the production process. Outsourcing in Sheffield is as old as manufacturing industry. How George worked at the very beginning can only be conjecture but what he could have done was to buy in 'blanks'. These are pieces of metal already cut into strips or made into bars and ready to be created into files. To make a file was a complex process.

Files were produced in all shapes and sizes according to the purpose for which they were intended. It is essential to use a high quality steel that will make a quick impression on the material that is to be filed and so that the tool's working surface does not become eroded. Large files from bars of steel that have been beaten into the requisite shape using a tilt hammer. In some places a steam hammer was used for the same purpose. The picture shows the tilt hammer at Abbeydale Industrial Museum, where agricultural cutting tools were made

The picture on the left shows the tilt hammer at the Abbeydale Industrial Museum, Sheffield.
It is thought that the expression 'at full tilt' meaning at full speed refers to working the hammers. as fast as possible

Larger files are forged from bar steel without undergoing tilt hammering (1). The square or flat files are shaped by means of a hammer and anvil whilst circular, half-round or triangular forms are made from bosses or dies fitting into grooves made for them on the anvil. The blanks are then placed in a large air-tight oven which prevents the steel oxidising but achieves the necessary softening or 'lightening' to enable the file to be serrated or toothed. The fire heats the oven until the blanks are up to the necessary 'red-hot' temperature and then the oven is allowed to cool gradually. If the metal is too soft the indentations may be too heavy or irregular and if too hard require a use of unnecessary effort to do the job. After being softened the blanks are carefully ground and smoothed down and are then passed to the file cutters.

FILE CUTTERS' SHOP.—W. HALL AND SON, ALMA WORKS.

Hand File cutting was usually done in long low workshops with as many windows as possible to give good light to help achieve accurate cutting. The picture is of the Alma Works of W. Hall and Son. When George Barnsley was at its zenith workshops may have looked like this though I doubt they had this many file cutters

The file cutter ties a blank on to the anvil in front of him, securing it with a strap that passes over each end of the file and is held tightly in place by the weight of his feet which are fitted into stirrups. The hammer that the cutter uses weighs from one to six pounds, according to the size of the file being worked. Its head is shaped to enable it to be pulled towards the workman while he is hammering. Similarly the chisel also made of very strong, tough steel varies according to the size of the file being fashioned. When the workman is cutting, the chisel is held in his left hand rather like a pen so that the hollow of his hand is turned towards himself. With each blow a tooth is cut and the blows are repeated in rapid succession until the whole surface of the file is covered, the file being moved as required by loosening the tread on the straps. Both sides are treated in this way but to avoid damage to the finished first side whilst the second one is being worked on, a flat piece of metal made of a mixture of lead and tin is put underneath. The finer the file required the higher the degree of accuracy required.

A common file is covered crosswise with a series of indentations running parallel to each other. The file cutter's sole guide is his experienced eye and steady hand in determining the distance between each cut, the cutting chisel being moved after each cut. According to size ten to twenty rows of cuts are required to cover the surface with teeth and there are sometimes more than a hundred teeth with in the space of an inch. '*Such files are bought for a few pence.*' (2).

To harden the finished product the files were 'laid on' with a mixture of flour, charcoal and salt water to prevent residues of lead clinging to the teeth. When dried the flour went white. It was essential they were dry or they would have exploded during the next stage when they were heated in a lead pot furnace to a high temperature. When withdrawn they were plunged into brine and then scoured to clean. They were then dried and wrapped in brown paper and stored for shipment around the world. The whole process of 'laying on' and using the lead pot furnace was a filthy job.

On July 2nd 1938 the *Sheffield Telegraph* featured 75 year old John Birkinshaw, *'the oldest and about the only hand "file-cutter" at work in a little shop in Ecclesfield where once some 400 people were engaged cutting files by hand in their cottages, little shops, gardens or backyards'.* He had left school when he was 10 to help his father and mother cut the files, which were taken by a donkey to Sheffield every Saturday. *'When he was a young man file-cutters had Monday as a day off for football practice, and little work was done before Thursday. Then they worked all night ready for Sheffield on Saturday.'*

John Birkinshaw's old workshop.
Note the windows to give maximum light.

I think it possible that George Barnsley's workshop in 1838 in Wheeldon Street was similar to the kind of workshops described above as being prevalent in Ecclesfield.

How did they get into files for shoemakers and leather workers? We can only guess. In a previous chapter I suggested that possibly he had the idea from Thomas Wing with whom he had served his apprenticeship. An alternative theory is that some of the files that he made proved suitable for shoemakers. In the *Dictionary of Leather-Working Tools c.1700-1950*, R.A. Salaman writes that **files** are *'one of the abrading tools used in the process of trimming and finishing. They vary in length from 3-12 in. (7.6-30.5cms).* He also states that shoe files are taken from the *'**ordinary range of metal-working files'**.*

I would speculate that if George Barnsley formed a good business relationship with one or two shoemakers or leather workers, it would follow that on his selling trips a customer might ask if it were possible to make a file that was shaped a bit differently in order to achieve some particular part of the shoe-making process. Alternatively the shoemaker might possess another kind of rasp made by another firm and George would be asked if he made or could make something similar. Eventually there would be a range of Barnsley files or rasps available. One shoemaker would tell another and George was then in a niche market. The illustration below shows a range of shoe rasps from the 1898 George Barnsley catalogue. Salaman also illustrates a Rand file, a knife-shaped file with file-cut teeth on one side and uncut on the other. It was used for trimming and levelling-up the edge of the sole. The safe edge or uncut edge prevented the shoe upper from getting damaged. Barnsley's definitely made Rand files as they are listed in their tool making chests in the 1927 catalogue. (See overleaf for photograph of page showing tool chests in 1927 catalogue)

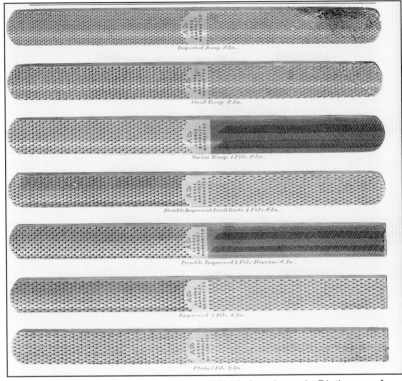

Shoe Makers Tools from Catalogue 1898. (as shown in Dictionary of Leather Working tools).
From top to bottom they are: Imperial Rasp, Oval Rasp, Swiss Rasp, 1/4 Double Improved Bevel Ends, Double Improved ½ file, Reverse, Improved ½ file, Plain Half file.
All are 8 inch.
Notice the trademark and George Barnsley name in the centre of each

Joan Unwin, archivist for the Company of Cutlers writes:
The mark of 'A' by a shoe was registered in 1854. I have looked at our records and none of the earlier Barnsleys who registered a mark used the symbol of a shoe. The George Barnsley who gained his Freedom in 1803 was granted the mark '2705'. From 1791-1814 almost all marks were given as sequential numbers.

It is unlikely that the George Barnsley who was given the mark 2705 was directly related to the George Barnsley who founded the firm, as the latter George's parents could not have married whilst the father was still an apprentice and they had had two children by 1803.

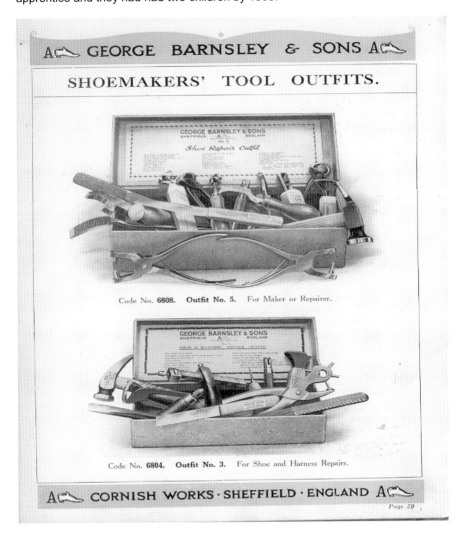

39

The Making of Knives

From trade directories by 1852 the firm's product range was listed as files, blades, awl blades, shoe, curriers' and tanners' knives. They had also become steel refiners. The shoe tool-making specialism involved my ancestor *Charles Barnsley,* brother of George. *Charles* is recorded on the 1861 census as a shoe blade hardener. There is further evidence of this specialism in the Sheffield flood compensation records (1865). Even after the move to Cornish Street they continued to outsource some of the work. They were paid £2 and 8 shillings compensation for '*4 gross of shoe blades lost, out grinding at Malin Bridge Grinding Wheel'.* (3). In 1864 J.Butler, T.Wild and German Wilson owned the Malin Bridge wheel.

The way a knife is made has been mechanised since the 1850s though the stages necessary are just the same as when they were made by hand. Apparently there are over seventy stages starting with the smelting of the metal. Today in a modern unit the process of getting the right proportions of carbon, chrome and tungsten are achieved by monitoring the process through computer analysis. Before the computer era this was done through experience and cold sample analysis. After reheating, the slabs of molten metal pass through the rolling mill where the rolling master ensures that the metal is spread to the correct width and length.

The finished sheets are then cut into 6-inch strips along the grain for maximum strength. A 25-ton power press blanks out the knife blades and a smaller press punches three holes for fixing the handle. The blade is then hardened at 820 degrees centigrade before being plunged into quenching oil. The blades are cleaned and kept straight in special racks before being tempered 4000 at a time in a special oven at approximately 300 degrees centigrade. The blades are then unclamped and ground. Grinding marks are glazed out and every blade tested for cracks and straightness and the back edge of the knife glazed.

Where wood is used to make the handles, the boards are cut into strips. The high-speed cutter shapes the two edges of the handles and these are cut into 4-inch lengths. A slot is sawed in for homing the blade and the front and back-end are shaped. Using a special jig (and these jigs vary for different types of knives), the three pinholes are drilled. The blade and handle are fitted together using pins that are then chopped off and squeezed to tighten.

To remove the roughness caused by the sawing of the handle it is sanded and then glazed to give a perfectly smooth finish before being bees-waxed to create a shine. It is then sharpened on helix wheels coated with a cubic boron nitride. The end product, the shoe knife, has to cut repeatedly through quarter inch thick leather. The knives are marked and the blades oiled before being packed into individual sheaths and boxed.

In a booklet bought in a second-hand bookshop some years ago, I found the following account, which claims to be compiled from journals and periodicals of the Victorian era. (4). I have included it here because in some ways it summarises the development of where Sheffield industry was at the time when George and *Charles* learnt their trades; that is 'the hearth sandwiched between dwellings' to the 'great manufactories' one of which was what George Barnsley and Sons became.

The most interesting branch of cutlery manufacture, as a process, is the initial business of forging…the forging of table-blades is a double-handed affair, the forger himself being assisted by a striker. The visitor to Sheffield will hear the ring of the forger's hammer not merely in the neighbourhood of the great manufactories, but in the place where he least expects it. He will come across a 'hearth' sandwiched between private dwellings in a quiet residential street and he will sometimes catch the rasp of the cutler's file in the dwelling house itself. It may be as well to explain here that the term cutler, now that the division of labour has given a specific title to every branch, is used in the trade in the restricted sense of 'putter together', that is, the man who fits the blade to the handle and produces the finished article. The solitary forger's hearth, discovered in a tranquil thoroughfare, might at first sight be easily mistaken for a small stable which had suffered a severe gunpowder explosion, but a second glance reveals the simple materials required to produce all that is essential in a good knife - a rod of steel, fire, hammer and water. Such are the elements out of which Mr Ruskin's 'masterful' magician will in a few moments present you with a table-blade, perfect in shape and symmetry, hard as adamant as to edge, pliable as a cane as to temper, and requiring only the grinder's touch and the cutler's hafting to be fit for the table. The forger's first operation is moulding (mooding as he calls it) or shaping which is done before the length of blade required is severed from the strip of steel, which he holds in his hand…

The straightening and marking are simple matters, but in the operation of hardening and tempering hand and eye have to be brought into delicate cooperation. Hardening is the process by which the steel blade is changed from the nature of lead to that of glass, from an obedient ductility to a petulant brittleness. This change is effected by plunging the heated blade into a vessel of dirty water, which stands by the anvil. The operation appears ridiculous in its simplicity but on its performance in the right way and at the right time depends the value of your knife. For this you have to rely on the trained judgement of the forger. Some tools will warp or 'seller', if they are not plunged into water in a certain way. Tools of one shape must cut the water like a knife; those of another must stab it like a dagger. Some implants such as files must be hardening in an old-standing solution of salt others in a stream of running water…the immersion of the knife into water is only momentary. When it is withdrawn the blade would snap like cast metal…. (Flexibilty) is obtained by 'tempering' or passing the blade slowly over the fire until the elasticity required is achieved. The degrees of ductility required are successively indicated by the changing colours appearing consecutively as follows: straw, gold, chocolate, purple violet and blue…elasticity is always obtained at the expense of the hardness of the steel.

References

(1)   Sheffield Local History Library (Mis. Paper 85L) Article from *The Working Man- a weekly record of social and industrial progress*, Saturday March 10th 1866 Vol. 1 No.10
(2)   Pawson and Brailsford's *Illustrated Guide to Sheffield and Neighbourhood* 1st pub. 1862. This edition 1971 pp.147-150
(3)   *Information on flood claims* http://extra.shu.ac.uk/sfca/ Sheffield University website searchable by name
(4)   Everett Michael D *Sheffield's Cutlers World of 1884* MDE Publication1986 pp. 15-16.

Chapter 5

Memories of people who knew the firm

I have tried to record these memories as individuals told them to me either in interviews face to face or over the phone or in letters. They are memories, in some cases shared after several decades, and they are coloured by the passage of time and by people's perceptions. This means there may be small inaccuracies but together they give a rich picture of life in a Sheffield tool-making firm which was unique but also representative of many other firms, a small number of which continue to make tools to this day.

Winifred Bentley b.1927

'Both my mother and father worked at George Barnsley's. My mother worked in the Globe Works' packing department prior to her marriage in 1923. My father worked on Cornish St from 1920 - 1940 approximately, making spikes for running shoes.

I used to watch my father work when I took him his dinner. I can see the place now, up the stone steps at the side of the clocking-in machine. It was right at the top where he and Mr. Williams, who lived on Addy Street, worked, using an anvil with bellows.

My father had an accident at work in 1930. One of the spikes he was working on hit him in the eye resulting in the loss of the eye. He received £100 compensation. I still have the bank-book.

Some years later my father developed cancer and died at the age of 40 in 1940. During his illness, Major George Barnsley used to visit my father at our home in Rutland Terrace. We had never seen a chauffer-driven car on our street! Major Barnsley used to bring him a bottle of sherry and half a dozen eggs as a tonic.

My mother remarried a man called Percy Frith who worked as a file hardener at Barnsley's until the 1950s.

These are my memories of George Barnsley's.'

Mr Lapper worked in 1943 as an apprentice for Vector Electrical Company, which was situated on Broadfield Rd. They did maintenance work and Mr Lapper was an apprentice electrician aged about 19 when the firm was employed by Barnsley's to convert the factory from the gas-powered engines to individual electric motors. There was one gas engine, which had a capacity of 250h.p. This powered a 3-foot wide belt from which ran shafting and counter shafting which consisted of several miles of belts powering tools such as hammers and grinding hulls.

He particularly remembers the little rooms that were file shops that were occupied by small numbers of very noisy girls.

The grandfather of Mr Lapper's wife was called John Spencer and he was a Barnsley employee. He was a file hardener and part of the process was to dip them in molten lead. William Stacey was Mrs Lapper's other grandfather and he was a hafter and worked mostly on butchers' knives. He was a proper cutler and always wore the traditional navy blue suit and bowler hat.

As he remembers it, the offices at that time were in the Globe Works and below the Globe Works was the caretaker's house that was occupied by an Albert Wallace.

Under the same roof as Barnsleys were several 'little mesters'. There was a family of grinders called Sambrook who gave Mr Lapper and his colleagues ten shillings (50p) each to fit the electric motor in his workshop on a Sunday so that he didn't lose any working time.

He also remembers Harrison's tableware was the next-door workshop to Harry Mortimer's leather workers.

Memories of working in the factory in 1943 include the discussions that were had over their sandwiches in the lunch-hour. Mr Sampson was a communist and William Stacey (Mrs Lapper's grandfather) a conservative. There were some strong differences of opinion and Mr Lapper just used to sit and listen.

He also remembers hearing about a man who was a 'little mester' working in Barnsley's in the 1920s or 30s. During the economic depression he gassed himself because of his lack of orders and the following day a job came in.

Eric Boocock

Eric grew up on Shalesmoor and at the time of talking to me he still worked in the cutlery industry for Crown Hand Tools Ltd. He retired in 2008.
Eric worked for George Barnsley and Sons from August 1984 until October 2002 as a scale tang cutler. When he applied for the job Henry Barnsley told him he was too old. At the time he was 40 and he responded by saying that they gave you a watch for twenty-five years service and he had that number of years left to work. He got the job. As it turned out he lasted longer than the firm, which during his time, reduced in number from twenty to three. Eric was one of the last three. By the end the conditions were terrible with receptacles catching the water that came through the roof when it rained and windows that fell out altogether when anyone attempted to open them. He also recalls how low the doors were from the bridges and that doors were narrow. It was difficult to get through them when he left his workshop if he was carrying a quantity of finished goods. The floors were also wood. The spiral staircase from the workshop was very low and the light switch was only at the bottom. There were also several massive cupboards in the building and by the end it felt very 'spooky'. Ropes hung from the roof. He recalled having odd experiences in the building such as being on the phone when the secretary was out and hearing the phone ring in another office and believing that he heard someone go to answer it even though there was no-one else on the premises.

In Cornish Street by the side of the double doors there is a patch of concrete. Here there was a stairway that went down into an underground passage that went under the building into what had been a WW2 air raid shelter. Some years previously the roof of this building was removed. (Colin Barnsley thinks this was to reduce the rates bill at the time).

Eric has memories of stocktaking every year. He can recall that every year some of the same products would still be there in exactly the same spot on exactly the same shelf. He particularly remembers two banana knives and on one occasion they found a 1947 newspaper. He felt that the tools were overpriced at the end when they were making two gross a day... 'designer prices being charged for stamped tools'. By the end he was doing the whole process. He worked towards the top of the building on his own in a workshop that was always known as Alec's shop. In essence it was a cutler's shop and it still had the fittings for gaslights. There was a door from the workshop on to a balcony and the lock on this door was a wooden lock.

Other employees that he remembers are John Revell who worked in the forge, Tony Mcdonald who did the stamping out and Mel Ripley; there was also a man called Dougie. Diane was the secretary. He always found Mr. Andrew to be fair with him but he did do some strange things like giving them all a week's holiday, the week he himself had to go into hospital. He bought a new press and to Eric's knowledge it cost about £25,000 probably more and was used about three times. According to Eric it seemed a big investment for so little use.

We did look during the interview at the reproductions in Salaman (1) from the old Barnsley catalogues. (Page numbers quoted below refer to Salaman).
There were several blanks for 'sweeps' (p.53) in stock but he never saw any produced during his time there. This was also true of punch pliers and punchers. In the early years before Eric's time awls were made and whilst he was there quite a variety of knives. All those illustrated on p.61 except for the hollow edge. He said that the broad knife was often used for some time by leather workers and then converted into either a breasting knife (p.64) or heel-paring knife (p.61). On page 64 he could not recall ever having seen a lace cutter made or a bottom-filling knife.
Hammers were still made, particularly the cordwainers, French pattern and German pattern (p.68-69) though he cannot remember ever seeing a 'closer's or paste fitter's pattern'(p.66) They also made some nippers (p.70).

Barnsley's tools were exported all over the world: New Zealand, Australia, South Africa, Germany, and Scandinavia. A lot went to the USA, particularly 'fleshing knives'. (These were used for removing the thin membrane on the flesh side of a skin called the areolar tissue so that the preserving oils could be applied and absorbed. (Salaman p.206). In addition knives went to India. The blade was flat and the cutting edge was slightly curved. (This was a tool used for pushing when paring shoe leather p.49). They also made knives for India that had big curved blades as seen in old films.

The firm did in fact have a trading relationship with R.W.Winning of Sydney, Australia from 1908 until it closed, though the relationship has continued between Winnings and Colin Barnsley's firm of Woodware Repetitions. Winnings acted and continue to act as agents and also stockists of Barnsley products for the subcontinent so the link between the two families has spanned more than a hundred years of trading.

Letter sent to me from Eric Feb 2008
'I have remembered some more about departments and people. I will do my best to write you a picture.
When I first went there you went in the front door on Cornish Street, passed the clocking-in clock and into a yard. First was Dougie's workshop round a corner and on the left hand side a storeroom where steel and blanks were kept. Across from that was a large shop that was empty though prior to the 1970s this was a grinding shop. I will come back to that later. Carrying on down the yard on the left were some steps leading up to the office that was above the warehouse. These steps were never used while I was there but were very close to the yard with assumed air-raid shelter. Then there was a gents' toilet on the left and on the right a grind wheel and forge then a big storage area for steel with a big steel door leading to Cornish Street. At the back of the area was a small door that was always kept locked at night but open in the daytime as that was where the shop called 'flying out' was. (A power press stamped out knife blades rapidly in steel) This yard was all open and led to the Globe Works entrance on Green Lane. Later there was a high wall built across this yard. Also across the yard was Fuller's and above that was our grinding shop and cutlers. We didn't go that way. We went through another doorway into that area and then up a spiral stair into the shop.
Turning right from the clocking clock round the side of Dougie's shop was a spiral stair leading up to the two walkways you know about and in this area there seemed to be more deterioration of the building fabric. In places there was hardly any mortar between the bricks. The caretaker's flat was in this area. There was a door leading to the yard. The flat fronted on to Cornish Street and was immediately to the right of the entrance to the works.

Departments and jobs
Flying out
This is the process of pressing out blades from sheet steel, punching holes in the tangs of shoe knives, lino knives, broad point knives, mill knives etc. Workers from Dougie's shop did all of these jobs along with the foreman from downstairs and later these jobs were done by Mel Ripley working entirely on his own.

Grinding wheel and forge
In the early years all grinding would have been done by hand on the big stones. In my time it would be jobs that were too difficult to do on the Morgan Fairest grinding machines.
John Revill and Tony McDonald would do the grinding and buffing and the glazing of blades such as butchers and fleshing knives etc. Tony would hand-forge Barnsley tools which were handmade from beginning to end using either a drop stamp and or a spring hammer.

Dougie's shop
Not too sure about this shop but I do know cutting nippers were assembled here and I think fleshing knives. They had a couple of other lads doing various jobs plus Doreen who I did see working a small lathe (I think facing up hammers though I understand that these were hand ground in the 1970s). A lady called Gladys Plant worked here as well as in the warehouse. I heard she had been there over 40 years.

Grinding shop and cutlers
In the grinding shop were Mick, Frank and Tony West when I first went there and probably others and later Mick's son Dave, Darren Jackson and Andrew Powell. They did grinding on Morgan Fairest machines, back, pointing, buffing and glazing of shoe knives, lino knives etc. All these people eventually left for better jobs or were sacked. Mick and Frank retired. When Mick retired we got another foreman called Donald. I can't remember his second name. Some of the younger lads were still there then.
In the cutler's shop was just Dave Vaughan and the work was piecework. When I joined him we did all the shoe, lino, broad point and mill knives. We did between 12 and 14 gross a week, each blade having back glazing, bore handle, locate, pin on, nip and rivet and sand if beech. If redwood, sand, fine glaze and dolly. All had to be whet then buffed again and they were then taken up to the warehouse.
We did have a gofer called Len Green who would take the work up for us and fetch work in that wanted doing. He also fetched up coke for us to use, as the only heating in these two shops was a pot-belly stove. Len retired after a couple of years and we got a young bloke called Clive.

Brightwork Warehouse
This was where finished work was taken and inspected for faults before being given to us for hafting in the cutler's shop. All the bradawls were knocked on and round-handled shoe, lino knives. The round handle had a single hole bored into them and the tangs were heated up, knocked on and pinned by whoever was available…mostly Doreen and later me. In the 1970s Gladys Plant had done this job. On the same level was a warehouse where all finished work was taken to be marked, oiled and boxed. Cutting nippers were hand-painted as were fleshing knives. Below this was a packing room where big boxes were packed to go out and the stock was kept in another part through locked doors. This floor level also had the offices. There were three in use though in earlier times there had been five. In one office there was a bust of George Barnsley who founded the firm.

People starting and leaving
Mr Henry Barnsley came to work on a daily basis in his late seventies and then stopped and only came now and again. He was eighty-four when he died. Andrew Barnsley (his son) ran the firm then with great help from Diane Birtles. Dougie had been there many years and had to take early retirement to look after his wife who was very ill. They didn't seem to replace him. People who were experienced set up for themselves. Annette left after a row with Mr Henry Barnsley about holidays. Gladys Plant I heard had been there about 50 years when she left. Later came a lady called Wendy and I think by

then Mick and Frank had retired and Donald came as foreman in the grinders' and cutlers' shop. Later Wendy and Donald became friendly and later got married. It was whilst Donald was foreman that the grinders' and cutlers' shops in the Globe Works were shut down and all the machines were moved into the big empty shop behind Dougie's old grinding shop and the cutlers into Alex's shop, a big shop at the top of the building above the office and warehouse. We moved all the machines ourselves. This involved lowering them on to flat beds with a chain-driven winch. Because the doors were too narrow we pushed them out on to Penistone Rd, then on Cornish Street and through the big gates into the shop. These machines came in pairs and weighed about half a ton each if not more and there were about eight altogether.

Lorraine left to go to America to live with her brother. Lorretta left and became a marriage guidance counsellor. Cathy from the office became a warehouse worker as was a lady called Joan. We were starting to get people coming and going after a couple of years…sometimes weeks or months. Since the shops were separated you didn't get to know them. Frank retired later than Mick and this was before Donald came. Mac left because of ill health and later John, Mick's son, for the same reason. Clive the gofer left after falling through the trap door leading under the air-raid shelter. His job was to fetch and carry empty bins and clean the toilets. When he went we took turns doing it ourselves on a rota. That started when there were nine of us and finished with the three of us. By this time all the warehouse ladies had gone including Cathy and Joan. A man called Billy Watson took over for about five years and then left and opened a fishing tackle shop.

We got a new foreman downstairs who lasted a year and another who lasted two weeks. We then got a man called Richard. By this time I think we had one in the warehouse, a man called Steve Drury who was there about five years. He left to be a carer for his mom. We then got a guy called Alan. We were then down to me, Dave Vaughan, Mel and Richard. Dave left and Richard opened a sandwich bar in Hillsborough. That left just me and Mel doing most of the jobs and Alan in the warehouse with Mr. Andrew and Diane helping to pack big cases. When me and Alan were made redundant, Mel was kept on to do odd jobs.'

Eric did recall one occasion when some particular tools were ordered and those supplied had the George Barnsley trade mark on them. The customer returned them and said that they preferred Oxley tools would they please change them. The management got Eric to buff off the Barnsley trademark and replace them with the Oxley. They were sent back to the customer who expressed appreciation of these Oxley tools as of a superior quality to those originally received!

During the 1990s Eric was asked by the management to keep a record of his work as a kind of marker of what could be achieved by one man in a day. He also wrote out from memory a list of knife-codes used in this work record. (See over page). 'Returns' sent back from the warehouse were tools which were still pitted after the grinder had supposedly finished them. Eventually Eric learnt to grind to avoid being laid off when work was scarce. At times of shortage of work some jobs were sent back from stock to be fully redone.

JOB #				JOB #			
DATE	AMOUNT	TYPE	TIME	DATE	AMOUNT	TYPE	TIME
1·6·92 MON	2GRS HO2 FROM 22·5·92			WHET	2GRS	"	7·45-9·00
LOCATE	"	"	7·45 - 8·15		2GRS HO2×H½C BEECH		
PIN ON	"	"	8·45 - 9·30	B/GLZE&POINT	"	"	9·00-9·30
NIP+RIVET	"	"	9·30-10·30	BORE HNDL	"	"	9·30-10·45
SAND	"	"	10·30-11·45	LOCATE	"	"	10·45-11·30
BUFF	"	"	11·45-14·00	PIN ON	"	"	11·30-12·15
WHET	"	"	14·00-14·45	NIP+RIVET	"	"	12·45-14·00
	2GRS 301/401×H½C ROSE			SAND	"	"	14·00-15·00
B/GLZE&POINT	"	"	14·00-15·30	BUFF	"	"	15·00-16·15
BORE HNDL	"	"	15·30-16·45	WHET	6 002	"	16·15-16·45
2·6·92 TUES	ABOVE 301/401		7·45-8·45	4·6·92 THURS	ABOVE HO2		
LOCATE	2GRS	"	7·45-8·45	WHET	1GRS 6 002	"	7·45-8·45
PIN ON	"	"	8·45-9·45		2GRS HO2×H½C BEECH		
NIP+RIVET	"	"	9·45-10·30	B/GLZE&POINT	"	"	8·45-9·15
SAND	"	"	10·30-12·00	BORE HNDL	"	"	9·15-10·30
FINE	"	"	12·00-14·15	LOCATE	"	"	10·30-11·15
DOLLY	"	"	14·15-15·30	PIN ON	"	"	11·15-12·00
BUFF	"	"	15·30-16·45	NIP+RIVET	"	"	12·00-13·45
3·6·92 WED	ABOVE 301/401			SAND	"	"	13·45-15·00
							P.T.O

Above a page from the notebook showing work done on a few days at beginning of June 1992.

Below the knife codes as remembered by Eric used in the work record.

KNIFE CODES

HO2c = H½ CLIP SHOE BEECH
HO9c = 4" CLIP SHOE POLISHED
306/40bc = 4" CLIP SHOE RED ROSEWOOD
19×5B = 5" BROAD POINT BEECH
19×5SFR = 5" SHEEPFOOT REVERSE BEECH
20% 1×5" FLAT BLADE NO HAFTING
301/40/c = H½ POLISHED ROSEWOOD HNDL
22×4" = DOGLEG CLICKER GREEN HNDL ROUND
215×OXLEY = H½C BEECH
310c = 4" ASH POLISHED (615CWEY)
900×4½ = ROUND BEECH HANDLE 2 PIN
5R×3½ RK = BREASTING KNIFE BEECH
19×6B = 6" BROAD POINT BEECH
HO2B = H½ BROAD POINT BEECH
211×3c = 3" CLIP BEECH
62H×4" = MILL KNIFE BEECH
216×H½ = HEEL PAIRER 2 PIN BEECH
212 OXLEY = 4" CLIP RND PRINTED BLACK HARE
2361 = SHOP KNIVES BEECH

992 = SMALL CRAFT KNIFE BLACK PRINTED HNDL
17×6G = FLAT BLADE ONLY
1948 = HAM SLICER WITH BEECH STALES
301×H½ VP = H½ HEEL PAIRER POLISHED WOOD RED
306×3c = 3" CLIP BEECH ROSEWOOD
62H×2½ = MILL & PIN BEECH
26×4" = 4" BUTT LINO KNIFE
19×H½ = 4" BROAD POINT BEECH
HO2×HO2B = H½ BROAD POINT BEECH ROUND
A89 = SMALL BLADE GREEN HANDL
O.C.2 = CLICKER BLADE ONLY
R53 CANNOT REMEMBER VERY RARE
183×OXLEY = H½ CLIP BEECH FOR TYPE
BEATRECO = TRADE BEECH

JUNE 13th 2010

Photographs taken by Eric Boocock 1990s

Mr Curtis (Doncaster) owns a 1983 Barnsley catalogue that his brother sent for in the 1980s because he used to do repair work on harness for horses. He preferred Barnsley tools. Mr Curtis himself worked until privatisation for British Rail. He recalls that many of the coaches were fitted with leather upholstery and the in-house workshops always used Barnsley tools for repairs and refurbishments.

Barbara Salvin is an administrator currently working in the Globe Works that were once owned by George Barnsley and Sons. Both her parents, James William Ogden and Lilian Ogden (nee Waterfall) whose picture is on the next page and Barbara's great aunt Louise Emmett worked for the firm. James and Lilian met at George Barnsley's and married on 18th December 1948.

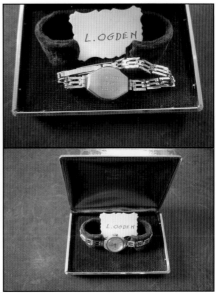

The handwritten label in the photographs above is the original and on the back of the watch is engraved
L.Ogden 1967 GB&S.

Lilian went to work at Barnsley's when she left school at 14. Her father already worked there. Lilian continued to work in the file department doing piecework even after Barbara was born and only left when her mother was ill. She wrote a short biographical summary to be read at her funeral in which she said: 'I served nearly 45 years here (Barnsley's) and enjoyed almost every minute of it. I wouldn't mind going back now at 80 but the firm's closed down!' She did in fact leave the firm just before the file department closed in the early 1970s. She did get the watch that marked 40 years service. In addition to the summary mentioned above she wrote her memories of the firm, reproduced at the end of this section.

Lilian was a file cutter and worked two machines at a time and produced round bastard six and 10" files. In the 1950s they always went to work in their stiletto heels. In the cold weather they would warm their hands in a milky white water that was in a big vat and used for washing the cut files. She also used to take some kind of special file to a 'little mester's shop' in Rosselle Street in Hillsborough for him to 'fine edge'.

As in all works of the period there was the usual fooling around and one man called Percy Wheeler caught a rat and hung it over the door to the kitchen so that all the women had to walk underneath it. During the midday break they used to play bingo with old-fashioned cardboard cards and a bag of numbers that were written on little wooden circles. They were not averse to a gamble on a horse and Lily's particular favourite was Red Rum. She also nipped out to buy sweets for everyone at dinnertime. They were such regular customers that they were allowed to weigh their own.

James Ogden aged 19. The picture was taken in a kiosk at Blackpool with 'a machine' that took your picture and told you your weight.
Jim is wearing two badges one is the Blackpool Tower badge, the other the Gloops club badge. Gloops was a cartoon character in the Sheffield Star, a local paper. Jim was nicknamed 'Gloops' because he had very fair hair.

James William Ogden was a file grinder working one of the very big wheels. On one occasion he was very lucky to escape with his life when his wheel burst. There must have been some slight warning as his colleagues shouted to him to move somewhere. Had he done so he would have been killed. In fact he hardly moved at all and obviously the bursting stone fragments missed him but landed where his colleagues had shouted at him to move to.

Lilian's father, Henry Waterfall, like many men in this period was a fisherman and belonged to the firm's fishing club. In 1938 he was presented with a cup for his success in a firm's competition.

Over the page, Henry Waterfall with his wife at Bradfield Rd, Working Men's Club
Left the Fishing Cup, note the firm's trademark of the A and shoe. The wording on the cup says:

PRESENTED BY P. T. BARNSLEY ESQ.
2ND H. WATERFALL
AUGUST 28TH 1938
WAINFLEET.

James Ogden was exempt from war service because he was making rasps for soldiers' backpacks and a tool for cleaning horses hooves. The latter seems a bit strange. Perhaps this was linked to farming and food production and perhaps local delivery transport was by horse-drawn vehicles? He was also in WW2 an ARP warden. According to family story he had to recover with another warden the body of a steeplejack who was killed whilst working on Barnsley's chimney. Barbara remembers being told that the body was on a roof. This would seem to be linked to the incident when a barrage balloon caught on the chimney but Colin's understanding was that the whole chimney came down as a consequence of a mistake and that this was what resulted in the death of three steeplejacks.

The only story that Barbara recalls from her great aunt, Louise Emmett concerns her walk to work. She used to come over Ball Bridge and one morning found the body of a young woman with long blond hair. She and her friend never went that way again.

When she was aged 80 Lilian wrote down her own memories of her time at the Barnsley works reproduced on the next page just as she wrote them.

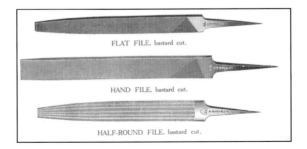

FLAT FILE, bastard cut.

HAND FILE, bastard cut.

HALF-ROUND FILE, bastard cut.

Memories of Bygone Days.

My name is Lilian Ogden nee Waterfall.
I worked for G. Barnsley + Sons File Trade from Jan. 1937
to March 19th 1973. I had some good friends and we got on
well together. I did different jobs my first one was laying
on files that was blacking or Whitening files ready to
be hardened by the man I worked for, it was hard work
for me as I was only small, I put on a furnace to dry
and he would put them one at a time in red hot lead
and dip them in, bosh of cold water, and send them up
on a lift to be scoured if they had to be sharpened my father
sandblasted them they were rinsed in 3 boshes of water
but it looked more like milk, they were dried on another
stove, + if they had on tangs on they were tempered + send
into the warehouse ready to be packed for orders.
From there I was put in the machine shop to start
cutting files, the machine was Hess machine the work was
3 to 10 and I enjoyed what I did My friends names were
Edith, Mary, Lily, Edna, Margaret, Rene Renee and Annie
but Annie marked the tangs on the files she wasn't a cutter
but I'm sorry to say theres only 3 of us left as far as I know
None of us earned a big wage as the prices were very poor.
I had two other machines to work on one was a little one
which looked on to the globe works I cut two at a time
as it was one that just did edges, part of the globe was hit
but one or two of the machines wer saved and put in the
big machine shop, no one was hurt as we had all gone home.
There wasn't many older ladies and they were G. K. Emma
Ellen, Edith, Lily, Gladys. The men got on with their
jobs. they were, Ernest George, Frank, Harry Joe, Jim, and
George the foreman also Jim another cutter, he was on Hess
machine and was the only man in the top shop. We worked
in there with tarpauling over the roof as the original

one was damaged and couldn't be put right till everything settled down. Before we moved to live on the Shirecliffe estate my Aunt Lizzie, Alice, Myra, used to go over ball bridge past the River Don and they saw a lady that had drowned, she was reared up at the side of a thick log at the side of the wall bigarettes were scarce during the war and I used to go through the globe to the tobacconist for 20 or 40 woodbines, we were lucky if we got 40, we smoked alsorts, for escample Players Weights, Park Drives, Pashas, there was some with a horse on but I can't remember the name, I nearly got caught one day, by the manager I was crossing one way and he was coming the other way I was lucky. I used to like a bet with Annie, the betting shop was next to the chip shop; the same row as the tobacconist. I go one day + Annie the next, we had vv's and doubles + we didn't do so bad. When it was a big race all the girls my age had a gamble + I used to write them all out. My Aunt came back to work in the warehouse setting the files for the hardeners, we used to go to a warehouse at the bottom of Hoyle Street, and the man used to let us weigh our own, everybody had a bag and it was a few pounds for him, only the women ordered not the men. We used to have a game of lotta at dinner time + a time it wasn't much when anyone won but it was a break, Everyone was piece work. There was a balloon put on some spare ground facing Ball Bridge but it broke away and got wrapped round the big chimney and we had to have steeple jacks to get it down, they had to go through the canteen roof to get to it but it cut through it all collapsed, Jim Ogden + Joe Powell had to get two planks and take a wheel barrow to get the men down

I think one was dead and two lived but I don't know what happened after wether another one died.

3

One young lad hung a rat outside the canteen + we had to
bend under it to go and
we weren't very pleased.   keep Mash our tea
we wore turbans sometimes, aprons, to our overalls clean
and I always wore high heels. Jim Ogden didn't go in the
army, I don't know if it was because he did shoe raps.
even we had to carry a card to prove we were exempt
from the A.T.S. and land army. All the men took it in
turns to fire spot. It was easy life but we were happy
                    By the way I married J. Ogden.
         I don't know what they called the boiler know there's one or 2
I can remember it was George who used to mend the belts
on the machines, and the man who looked after the
boiler to keep the steam going.

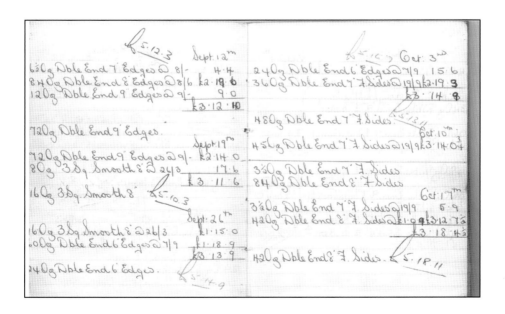

A page from Lily's work record book, showing her piecework weekly
earnings in 1966.

55

Lily and friends. It is possible to see their growth from teenagers to women. Lily is the one in the lightest coloured overall in the pictures on the left and towards the middle

Mr Brian Armstrong has vague recollections of his grandfather, Mr James Martin Armstrong, who came from Belfast where he was an ironmonger. He moved to Glasgow at some time and Brian remembers staying with his grandparents there in 1942. As Brian understood it, his grandfather was the representative covering Scotland and Ireland for George Barnsley and Sons. He did not know his grandparents well because of the distance they lived from Sheffield.

Newspaper cuttings
The 3 pictures below are cuttings kept by one of the Barnsley family. It is
believed that they are from a Sheffield local paper in 1972 and they were
sent in to the paper by Lily Booth who was probably one of the firm's
workers or retired workers. The pictures probably date between WW1 and
WW2. She said that the picture immediately below was a fishing club outing.

Photographs taken by Colin Barnsley in 1974

File grinding machine shop showing one trough.

Above from yard looking towards front door and showing caretaker's flat and doorway to the ground floor stockroom. Below Doug Allison's machine tooling shop. Doreen in foreground

Above, inside of Oxley's section when products were finished. Workers were Mary and Agnes. Below, show blanking, knife hardening and temporing shop including gas fired conveyor-fed hardening machine

Alec Alcock's knife grinding shop

Photographs loaned by Tom Alcock

Alec Alcock, manager of the grinding shop. He was a
keen gardener!

Women workers: Rita top right, Agnes in front of Rita,
Mary next to Agnes.

References

(1) Salaman R.A. *Dictionary of Leather-working tools c.1700-1950 and the tools of
allied trades,* London George Allen and Unwin 1986

Chapter 6

Awl Department Wages Book 1892-94

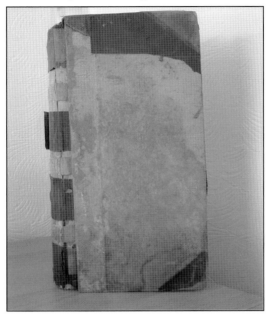

This book was rescued from a skip in the early 1980s. It is a large ledger, measuring approximately 13 inches by 6 inches and is about 2 inches thick with the inscription inside the front cover 'Awl Blade Departments Work Book October 31/92' (1892). The book offers the facility for the wages' clerk to have a list of the department's workers arranged alphabetically with a reference to where their wage record starts in the book. For example James Allen's records started on page 110, Sarah Scamadine's on page 310 though this system was not kept up to date.

As in most trades in Sheffield at that time the workers were on piecework that was almost self-employment. The wages as can be seen in the illustration below, were worked out according to quantity of artefacts completed. In most of the light metal industries there was a fixed price worked out with the unions for completion of a particular process on particular items. The records below shows the price per gross was recorded and next to that the number produced and the amount earned. So for making Barnsley heel awls, workers were paid four-pence halfpenny a gross and therefore for 4 gross earned one shilling and sixpence. The total earned during the week was then added up and a total shown. Some deductions were made which indicate what seems to me to be a bit of the 'self-employment' feel which was probably residual from earlier days when people hired wheels along the rural valleys around the Sheffield area. Wheel rent of one shilling and two pence was deducted from the gross amount earned and a gas charge of four pence a week was made. A final deduction of 10% of the gross wage was made on certain items. Colin Barnsley believes that this was an amicable agreement between the Barnsley family managers and the workers to keep prices down in order to try to beat the recession of that decade.

Below is a scanned image from the awl book, which illustrates that L. Ashmore earned six shillings and ninepence halfpenny. Wheel rent was one shilling and two old pence and there was a charge for gas of four old pence making the deduction in the right hand column of one shilling and five old pence. The 10% deduction is shown on the gross amount for the first 3 items.

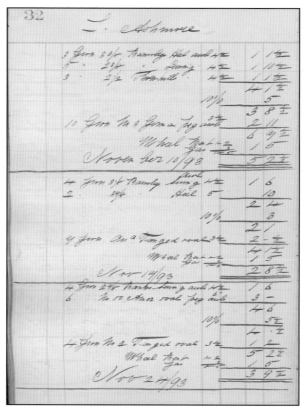

Sometimes different parts of the process of making an awl blade are recorded, such as forging, bending, marking, hardening, often on the same man's record for the week; other entries are simply for the total number produced. Finishing tends to be women's work and was probably the final polishing process. Their wages were much lower so that they took home less than half the pay of the majority of the men.

In the wages book, the different types of awls made during this period include saddle stitching, harness, buckling, Barnsley heel, California sacking, tang oval peg, clicker and collar to name but a few. The picture below from a catalogue of the period shows some of these as well as others that were part of the Barnsley patterns.

Looking at the names of the workers it appears that members of the same family were involved in the same trade. This would suggest the usual pattern of the late nineteenth century of father teaching son or at least father getting son or daughter an apprenticeship in the firm. We have Arthur Clay and Henry Clay and E.Turton and Miss P Turton. I would guess that there were family dynasties of several generations working for the firm from the early years of its existence until well into the twentieth century and the beginning of decline. Names of some of the workers whose wage records are included as members of the awl department are: Ashmore, Butler, Clay, Lavender,Taylor, Scamadine.

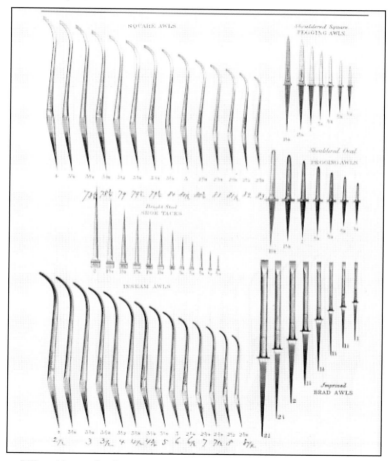

Different types of awls reproduced from a page in the firm's 1898 catalogue as reproduced in R.A. Salaman's Dictionary of Leather Working Tools.

References

The wages book is currently in the keeping of Peter Machin, a local historian.

Chapter 7

The Buildings - Cornish Works

Cornish Works is an integrated site in Cornish Street occupied for approximately 150 years by George Barnsley and Sons. George Barnsley and his brother *Charles* bought the first part, a steel-making concern on Cornish Street from Isaac and Edwin Inman, two brothers born in Stannington. The total area was 1040 square yards,' which said parcel of land contains in the whole 1040 square yards and steel furnaces, workshops and all other erections and buildings'. (1) [Also see Appendix 1]. All the buildings fronting Cornish Street date from the 1850s to the 1880s. During this period there was considerable development and some mechanisation. The buildings fronting Cornish Street include the caretaker's house, offices and workshops.

Book QU page 385 entry 416 registered Jan 25th 1851 at 2 in the afternoon

A memorial to be registered of an indenture bearing the date 23rd Jan 1851 made between Isaac Inman of Sheffield, steel melter of the first part, Edwin Inman, farmer of Sheffield of the second part, George Barnsley of Sheffield aforesaid, file manufacturer of the third part, and Charles Barnsley of Sheffield, cutler of the fourth part.

Of and concerning all that piece or parcel of land situate in or near to a certain street in Sheffield heretofore called Cleakham Wheel Rd but now called Cornish St containing in its abuttal on the northeast partly on the said street called Cornish St and partly on a certain public road there 73 feet or thereabouts; in its abuttal on the southwest on furnaces belonging to Thomas Holy Beard, John Jones and Thomas Cockayne 71 feet; in its abuttal on the northwest on land and premises belonging to James Dixon Esq 123 feet and its abuttal on the southeast on other premises of the said Thomas Holy Beard, John Jones and Thomas Cockayne which have been agreed to be demised to William & Samuel Butcher 132 feet and which said piece or parcel of land contains in the whole 1040 square yards and the steel furnaces, workshops and all other erections and buildings. The execution of this indenture by the said Isaac & Edwin Inman is witnessed this day by James Wilson and Thomas Gould of Sheffield gentlemen and the execution by the said George Barnsley and Charles Barnsley is witnessed by Samuel Stones & George Angus both of Sheffield, clerks

The picture left shows the original part of the building purchased by George and Charles in 1851.

The caretaker's flat is on the ground floor at the front of the four-storey building in Cornish Street and to the right hand side of the entrance to the yard, which was wide enough to take what in earlier days would have been a cart, and in the twentieth century a motorised vehicle. Above it is a lintel carved with the firm's name. This was added at a later date than the original building, probably at the time when George Barnsley b.1837 joined his father 'formally' in the business which would have been about 1859 when he was 21 years old.

According to an industrial archaeological survey done in 1998 (2) the 1851 ordinance survey map shows that the site that became Cornish works was a range of buildings with a cart entrance from Cornish Street, a narrow yard with further buildings to the side and the rear and four circular cementation furnaces. By 1890 the works had been developed so that the original yard has been encroached on and the cementation furnaces replaced by other buildings. The circular industrial chimney in the yard on this map indicates that the site was mechanised by this time.

The Chimney

This chimney was destroyed in November 1940 during WW2. In Chapter 5 Lily Ogden mentioned this incident in her handwritten memories, as her husband in his capacity as an ARP warden brought one body off the roof. Her daughter, Barbara thinks it was the body of Jim White as Lily always said it was a young man with a young family. A barrage balloon cable became caught around the chimney. A steeplejack firm was called in. On the Friday they erected ladders on the outside of the chimney. At the inquest a witness stated that they had considered cutting the cable then but had decided not to do so because of the risk of leaving a trailing cable. It was also near to blackout time. On the Saturday three men went up the chimney to release the cable but the tension on the cable overnight had increased the strain on the chimney. As soon as instructions were given for the motor winch to draw in the cable it had only moved a few inches when the men up the ladders on the chimney shouted that the chimney was down. The cable did not break. The witness had expected the cable to slide round the chimney as it was drawn though. He was unaware that the men were still up the ladders. William Edward Harrison a partner in the firm said that he had seen the cable round the top fifteen or sixteen feet of the ninety foot chimney but from the ground it was impossible to tell how the cable had become entangled. The initial inspection by the three men on the Friday had revealed that the cable had cut into the stone coping and also into the iron band supporting the chimney lower down. On Saturday he was himself in Dixon Street when he saw the top thirty feet of the chimney fall. (Dixon Street ran between Penistone Rd and Cornish Street). Given the height of the chimney the view from Dixon Street may have been the best vantage point he could find from which to see the top of the chimney. He rushed round to the works to find Charles Haywood (aged 57) under a pile of bricks and debris and Harry Brindley (aged 40) and Jack White (aged 24) on the roof of a workshop. All were badly injured and died from those injuries, three civilian casualties amongst many in Sheffield and elsewhere who died as a consequence of the Second World War. The coroner brought in a verdict of accidental death believing the chimney collapsed through pressure from the wind and the pulling by the winch. With what seems to me to be a surprising conclusion he added that there was no negligence on the part of anyone concerned! Colin's father, Fred Barnsley told him that because it was wartime the incident was 'hushed up'. No coroner's report exists, as the records were lost in the Sheffield Blitz. (3).

The current manager of Harrisons' steeplejacks, Mr Harrison, having checked their records believes that a repair job was done to the top of the chimney but can find no records of the chimney being taken down.

Changes to the building 1885
There are planning documents in Sheffield Archives dated May 1885 indicating that some development was planned for part of the Cornish Works. These plans submitted to the Sheffield Planning Department did lead to some changes to the building. (4).

After the death of the founder's eldest son George in 1895, the firm was managed by the last of the four sons of the founder, Henry. He had a turbulent few years during which he 'sold' the buildings to his nephew and then bought them back. (See page 127). A possible theory given by a retired accountant consulted by Colin as to why Henry took this action is that the mid 1890s were a time of depression and Henry might have feared bankruptcy. If his nephew owned the buildings they could not in the event of bankruptcy be used to pay off liabilities. It seems surprising after a few years of depression that he should then in November 1901 make the decision to expand by purchasing the land and buildings adjoining Cornish Works, which were and still are generally known as Globe Works. Even when rented out this was a very big commitment. (See end of chapter for copy of relevant deed).

100 years later
Looking at the building from Cornish Street the General office in the 1950s and earlier was straight ahead of the main entrance but on the first floor. On the same floor were the directors' offices for Colonel George Barnsley and Percy Barnsley on the yard side. The export office was on the front overlooking the street. The accounts office was at the left hand end of the same floor. The hoist at the main gates served all floors. At the very top of the building was the handle garret (store rooms). The packing/dispatch room

was to the right on the first floor. All the warehousing of knives and tools was on the floor above. The file department covered the ground floor. Moving towards Green Lane there is a strange double wall with a tapered gap between it and the road wall. This was a crucible furnace wall containing 22 pots. Almost at the end of the works was the steel warehouse near the gate that does not have on it the firm's name. Different grades of steel were mixed in this warehouse, prior to melting. The next doorway was the last part of the building to be added to the works.

Going round the back to the area behind the Globe Works buildings were some workshops rented by individual work people. There were Ron Jackson, the wood turner, Mr Brown who was the last hand file cutter in Sheffield who was cutting special rasps and Mr Sambrook, a hand grinder. A little further along was Fuller's, a chisel company.

In the picture to the left, Fuller's occupied the ground floor of the building to the right and the upstairs of the building on the left.
In the 1970s Oxley's shop was above Fuller's in the building to the right

This picture is taken standing almost in the same place. Fuller's building is on the right. The white building is the back of the main office. The jagged roof in the 1990s became the 'new' grinding shop but had been the file grinding and cutting shops which had to have a new roof after WW2.

To the left of the arch is part of what would have been Fullers' shop. The central building in the picture was the Barnsley forge and the hand grinding shop is the building on the right where buffing and glazing were also carried out. Buffing and glazing wheels were made of wood and felt and were dressed with glue and grit of various grades, 60,80 and 120 depending on the job. The higher number was for finer work. In later years 'coldax' cement was used instead of glue.

The boarded-up workshop on the right of the picture (above) was the' flying out' workshop used for stamping out blades, punching holes in tangs, hardening and tempering. In the 1990s this was known as Dougie's workshop and by the time the firm closed it was Mel Ripley who worked here. To the left is the back of the steel warehouse. In the background is the Dixon's Cornish Place building showing upstairs windows and chimney. Nature is reclaiming the derelict buildings.

The picture shows the remains of the exhaust pipe from the engine room at the back of Globe Works. The engine powered a considerable amount of the machinery.

Sadly there are no known photographs of the buildings that show it when it was a highly productive and successful business. The nearest we have is the line drawing which appears in the early catalogues and shows other nearby buildings

CORNISH WORKS,

SHEFFIELD, ENGLAND.

Extract from deed concerning the purchase of Globe Works 1901:

Description of Lands: All that piece or parcel of land situate lying and being in Cornish St bounded on or towards by land now or formerly belonging to Edward Grantham & Henry Isaac Dixon and demised to Thomas Staniforth on or towards the east by the River Don on or towards the south by other land now or formerly belonging to Joseph Roberts & Alexander Roberts the younger and on or towards the west by Cornish St aforesaid and which said piece of land contains in the whole 380 superficial sq yds and is more particularly delineated in and described by the plan drawn in an indenture of lease dated 13th Sept 1879 made between the said Edward Grantham & HI Dixon of the one part and Unwin & Rodgers Ltd of the other part and therein coloured pink.
And also all that warehouse or engineer's manufactory and all other erections and buildings on the said piece of ground.

Parties: William Needham Longden Champion formerly of Cantley Hall, Doncaster but now of Reddleworth Hall, Norfolk, Esq & Francis Beresford Champion of North Pickenham, Norfolk, Clerk in Holy Orders of the one part and Henry Barnsley of Cornish Works, Cornish St, Sheffield, cutlery manufacturer of the other part

Description of Land
First. All that piece or parcel of land situate in the Township of Sheffield bounded on or towards the southwest by Penistone Rd on or towards the south partly by a street there called Green Lane and partly by hereditaments belonging to Messrs Steel & Garlandon or towards the east partly by a road leading to the River Don known as Cornish St and partly by hereditaments occupied by the said Henry Barnsley and on or towards the north and northwest by the hereditaments next therein described and containing in the whole 3330 superficial sq yds or thereabouts the shape position and dimensions of which are delineated in the plan drawn on the first skin of an Indenture dated 18th Jan 1872 made between Philip Henry Unwin of the one part and William Kirkby Peace & Alfred Buckingham Ibbotson trustees of the Chantry Building Society of the other part and thereon coloured green
And secondly all the piece or parcel of land adjoining the last described and bounded on the southwest by Penistone Rd on the northeast by hereditaments belonging to Henry Barnsley to the

southeast by land first hereinbefore described on or towards the northwest by hereditaments formerly belonging to Mr Bagnall but now to Mr George Clark and containing 1413 superficial sq yds the shape position and dimensions coloured pink in the said plan together with all the numerous buildings and other erections. And also that messuage or dwelling house and the warehouses, counting offices, workshops, grinding wheels, hearths, coach houses, stables and sheds. Also the steam engine with three boilers thereto and the pulleys and shafting connected therewith. Also all the mill gear, shafts, pulleys, drums, machinery etc belonging to the said William Needham Longden Champion & Francis Beresford Champion and which are now fixed or used in or about the said premises which altogether are known by the general name of the GLOBE WORKS and are now occupied by the vendors or their tenants (5)

References
(1) Land registry *Documents Book QU* page 385 entry 416 registered January 1851.
(2) Cornish Works: *Notes from RCHM* England (copy RCHHE 199900).
-NBR Index No. 98222,
-NGR SK 3484 8830
-Survey !9th Oct 1998
(3) Report from *The Star, Shefffield,* Friday November 29th 1940, thanks to Jean White, daughter of Jack White, one of the steeple jacks who died.
(4) CA 206/7400 Microfiche Aperture card.
(5) Deed dated 11th Nov 1901 Volume 48 page 23 entry 13 Registry of Deeds, Wakefield.

Chapter 8

Hard Times: the decade following WW2

It is necessary when considering a firm such as George Barnsley's to recognise that there are times when the whole historical, social and political climate of the period will impinge heavily on the capacity of any individual firm to develop. This was particularly true in the twentieth century following both world wars. The aftermath of WW1 included a lengthy economic depression. This was not so much the case following WW2 but there was a serious shortage of materials including steel. Even in 1956 the minutes of the Barnsley directors' meetings include a reference to the fact that they lacked a regular steel supply and that this was outside the company's control. This firm amongst others in cities throughout the UK had also suffered war damage

Other factors included exports being hit by other countries imposing import duties. Australia's import duties imposed in 1951 badly affected the Sheffield cutlery industry. It is also true that generally speaking the general ethos and organisation of many of Sheffield's cutlery and tool-making firms was Victorian. Many were relatively small family firms and the management skills required in the developing modern industrial world were in many instances unsuited to the challenges that faced them. They lacked capital to invest in modern machinery and many family firms lacked marketing skills and the capacity to see how they could adapt to the rapidly changing times. The Sheffield name alone was no longer enough.

In Sheffield, firms like Barnsley's depended on their name as a supplier of high quality tools but within another decade their markets were being invaded by manufacturers in countries like Japan where production costs were much less. This was partly due to cheaper labour costs but also to more mechanised processes. By the end of the 1960s production of cutting tools in the Far East cost less than the Sheffield firms had to spend on raw materials.

The need various craftsmen had for specific kinds of tools grew less. This was because different materials and more mechanised processes came into being and many firms failed to adapt their skills to produce products that would continue to be needed. Obvious examples are a discontinuing need for scythes when machines harvested the grain. The more easily and cheaply produced paper carrier bags and eventually plastic bags largely replaced traditional baskets woven from natural materials that required special cutting tools. Slowly but surely this applied to the British boot and shoe industry that declined rapidly after WW2. The knock-on effect must have impinged on the George Barnsley firm the bulk of whose business was the production of tools for shoemakers and leather workers.

A Selection of Minutes of Directors' Meetings 1946-56

The minutes that I have been able to study are for some of the directors' meetings, which took place during this period. The overall feeling that I had as I read them is one of struggle. It was a struggle to keep the business on track as it was for any manufacturing firm in the post war period. There were differences of opinion between directors who were members of the Barnsley family over the issues arising. The chair was Colonel George and the other directors were Mr Percy, Mr George junior, Mr Fred and Mr Henry. Mr Wheatcroft was a financial adviser and a Mr Staton was in attendance as secretary. Contributions from the family members are recorded in the minutes in the time honoured way by reference to them as Mr. followed by their usual first name.

It seems that Mr Henry was in essence responsible for administration and finance though that title is not given to him anywhere in these minutes, Mr. George junior seems responsible for sales and Mr Fred for the management of some of the departments: A and B.

During this ten year period there seems to be some recurring themes. As I see them these are: salaries and wages, maintenance of the building and plant, new technology, staffing levels, orders and production and obviously, the balance sheet.

Salaries and Wages

In 1946 the directors found it difficult to agree on their own salary structure but finally agreed on a format that was a classic compromise!

Towards the end of 1952 the engineers had been awarded a pay increase of 7/4d a week. It was proposed to extend this to the whole of the workforce towards the beginning of 1953.

In April 1956 Mr Henry informed the meeting that all the men on the works had received a pay rise of 12/4d per week and that it had been recommended that the lighter trades should receive 15s a week for all men aged over 25 years and 9/6d a week for women over 21. It was therefore agreed (rounding up to pounds) that these men should receive an increase of £40 per annum and 'that Skelton should receive a pro rata increase'. The women concerned would receive increases of £26 per annum and juniors pro rata increases all dated from April 2nd 1956.

Staffing

In 1946 Mr Henry was given permission to take on a girl aged about 15 for clerical duties as Mrs Allen an existing employee wished to revert to half-time employment. Mr Percy died in 1951 and was not replaced on the board of directors. I suspect that he was a considerable loss to the board in terms of the balance of power. He seemed to be a moderating influence in many of the meetings when positions were becoming entrenched.

New Technology

In 1946 the directors authorised the purchase of a new plate machine for Mr Cutts' department at an expected cost of £70-£100. In 1952 an issue arose over time clocks. It was proposed to install more time clocks in different parts of the works. However this had proved difficult because there was a lack of parts to adapt the old clock. A new clock had therefore been ordered and was expected in two weeks and at intervals in the future new clocks working off the master clock would be installed in other parts of the works. Also in 1952 Fred reported that a new precision lathe had been installed in B department costing £218.15 and was 'a very great benefit'. In addition a new whet machine was being built which would be able to deal with most patterns of blades. This would release a hand grinder for more hand-ground work when required.

It was reported to the directors in April 1956 that Miss Brookes who had been with the firm for 33 years would be leaving in the summer and it was therefore proposed to give her a 'leaving present' of £100. Miss Brookes retirement led Mr Henry to propose that they spend £700-800 on office equipment machines in mechanised book-keeping in order to expedite the getting out of statements, balances etc. and also to save on salaries. He was given permission to look further into this and to report back to the next meeting. The result was a recommendation that they bought the Burroughs 'Sensimatic' accounting machine. Henry with illustrated sheets reported as follows:

At present it takes a week to get out invoices. This could perhaps be somewhat overcome by a very experienced staff, but the company does not have such a staff. The result was delay in sending out statements and therefore in getting in cash…If the board decided to purchase, Mr Henry could do with one less on the staff in the accounts office and as Miss Brookes was to retire he would not replace her. The saving would be £300 per annum. The price of the machine was £781 and he had placed an order subject to confirmation by the board. It was agreed to buy the machine.

Maintenance of the building and plant

At the meeting at the end of 1952 there is a certain amount of evidence that the financial position is not as healthy as they would like. Mr Henry agreed to look into the possibility of making a claim to the War Damage Commission re a bill already in for £1250 and for another bill to do with damaged plant for £711. They did not hold great hope of getting this money. However in 1953 the claim for £711 was paid and with interest came to £ £836 7s 7d. Progress had been made on the larger amount and Mr Henry reported that at least some of it would be paid but he did not know how much. They did agree to write off 50% of this expenditure at the end of the year if it had still not been paid. In 1952 painting a further section of the works was deferred until the spring of the following year. In the same year there had been a proposal to install a new hoist in the yard but an alternative suggestion of levelling the yard so that things could be more easily rolled was agreed though was not acted upon despite the report in October 1953 that all deferred repairs had been completed. Perhaps levelling the yard was not strictly speaking considered a repair. In August 1956 Mr Fred asked that an outside contractor be brought in to do roof repairs as the roof was leaking in several places. This was agreed to.

Orders and production

In 1952 Mr George junior reported that there had been a fall off in sales due to recession in the textile industry and also in the motor trade. The hope was that this was only temporary. The new catalogue which recorded a new telephone number (see note at end of chapter) had brought several new enquiries and orders. Several customers let them have free space in private exhibitions because the Barnsley firm could supply show boards and tools on a sale or return basis as well as on some occasions a representative in partial attendance.

In New Zealand the representative had opened business with Briscoe a former customer and an order was expected. It was hoped that as tools were not classed as luxury items an order would be coming through soon. The original customer in India for a consignment of files had refused payment but two other possible openings were in view and it was hoped that this would be settled in the next three weeks.

In Mexico sales of shoe knives had suffered a temporary setback because of the imposition of import duty. They were making moves to try to find a way round this obstacle.

Mr Fred reported that A department was now carrying a reasonable stock in hand except for 2405 Lino knives production which was delayed waiting for steel that had to be rolled. B department had most tools in stock except for three lines of pincers and cutting and tower nippers (size 2) which were in the process of being forged.

There was a recognition that the improvement in building up stock has been achieved because of the fall off in orders and that this lack of orders must be tackled as a priority. They recognised the need for appropriate balance between sales and production but no indication of how such a balance was to be achieved was agreed. A summary of total sales (knives, tools and files) is supplied for 1950-52. From Jan-Dec 1950 £96,475, Jan-Dec 1951 £102,122, Jan-Nov 1952 £90,104 and it was noted that shoe rasp sales were down badly because of lack of travelling.

In October 1953 Mr George junior reported that despite the difficulties in the post war period customers had been loyal because of the high quality of the products. He commented that this was due to the production managers. At the same meeting Mr Fred reported that production was keeping up with orders though they could do with increasing the stock of cutting nippers. Col. Barnsley commented that it was essential to try to build up stocks even more because costs were going to rise and having stock in hand would be to the benefit of the company. In October 1953 sales were down by just over £7000. It was thought that this was because of Australian import restrictions and a shortage of cash in internal markets. People who wanted knives wanted them quickly and only ordered a few at a time so that they were not carrying tools in reserve. 'In other words they were making the supplier (G.B.& S Ltd) carry the stocks.' At that time they were carrying £25,000/£26,000 worth of stock.

In the October 1953 meeting there was discussion about the possibility of advertising at the Canadian International Fair to be held in Toronto in 1954. Mr Henry thought Mr George junior should go to Canada for three or four weeks and represent the company at the fair and try to find a good agent who would work in Canada on behalf on George Barnsley's. It was agreed to spend £100 advertising at the Fair and to visit Roebuck's in London to gather further information about it with a view to making a decision at the January meeting.

In August 1956 Mr Henry was concerned about turnover in A department. There was a problem of a lack of a cutler and Col. Barnsley was taking this up and hoping to obtain a trainee. Despite these concerns sales were up £1000 on the previous year whilst in B department they were down over £1300. Questions were raised about running spikes but it was planned to get these off as soon as possible 'in case of trouble in the Middle East and Suez Canal'.

In August 1956 Mr Henry felt that the turnover in F department should be £31,000 for the first six months of the year when in fact it was about £5000 short of that. Part of the problem was the shortage of labour and also the difficulty of steel supply. They had however now managed to secure a stock of billets.

The balance sheet
At the end of 1952 the over-all balance fluctuated between debit and credit but was gradually settling down to an overall credit. In October 1953 there was in the general account a surplus of £4719 and in the No. 2 account £2036. Debtors amounted to £18,727. By April 1956 there was little change in the main bank account. This was in credit to the amount of £4238 whilst No 2 account was in credit to the amount of £3073 though some of this was ear marked for payment of tax.
They were also in April 1956 facing a substantial rise in rates and Mr Henry had already notified all tenants that it would be necessary to increase rents from April to meet the rise. In August 1956 income looked like being about £1000 more than the previous year.

The meeting held January 1956
I have singled this meeting out, as it is the one that in my perception shows serious tensions between different members of the board. It is recognised early on in the meeting that although income was up in 1955 to £106,000 this was a result of higher prices rather than turnover. It was essential therefore to increase turnover or to reduce overheads.

Both Col. Barnsley and Mr Henry comment that the orders are there to increase sales but Fred who was production manager of A and B departments pointed out that he could not achieve this because of the shortage of cutlers and steel and as rolling steel was outsourced he could do nothing about this. Col. Barnsley asked if the union had been approached about another cutler. Mr Fred's response as recorded in the minutes was 'No!' The way this is recorded in the minutes suggests it was expressed from strong feelings. Mr Henry commented that if they could get another cutler it would not be policy to set him on until the steel situation were resolved. There is no further discussion of this in the minutes. Col. Barnsley in the chair does not seem to have pursued it any further. It is almost as though Mr Henry's pronouncement was accepted without question.

Mr Wheatcroft the financial advisor asked how file prices compared with other companies. Mr George said very favourably with other English companies but German prices were lower. The company held its own because of its reputation and quality products. Mr Wheatcroft asked if turnover could be increased by £10000 in 1956. Mr Henry replied that it depended on regular steel supply and that was outside the company's control. Again no other member of the board expressed an opinion.

The next issue impinged more on Mr Fred's everyday working life than on that of the others. A Mr Beeley who had been in a management role in B department had died and Col. Barnsley suggested that to cut down on overheads he should not be replaced. Fred disagreed and suggested training a younger man which I presume would have saved something on wages. No one seems to have responded to that. Col. Barnsley asked if Edna was pulling her weight and Mr Fred said yes in that she started half an hour before the office staff. Henry said she was now but hadn't done so when Mr Beeley was alive. Col Barnsley repeated that to restore bonuses economies had to be made and therefore Beeley would not be replaced. It was left to Mr. Wheatcroft to ask if Mr. Beeley's loss had been felt to which Mr Fred replies 'Yes, a lot'. He reiterated that he could not manage without a replacement because everyone was up to the limit of effort and Edna was only willing to continue until there was a replacement as her health was not good and she was feeling the strain. Someone else had to be found or trained as he had already stated.

Mr Henry said that it should not be necessary for two people to be concerned in management of A and B department to which Mr Fred responded that he also had to give time to looking after C department as well. (C department was probably curriers and tanners but had been absorbed into A and B by the 1970s). The issue was shelved by suggesting that Mr Henry, Mr Fred and Mr. Wheatcroft should meet to go into this further.
The final item on the agenda was Col. Barnsley asking if the stock books were ready. Mr Henry said he was still waiting for A department to which Mr Fred replied that he had no time to do these in working hours and that he was working on them at home at night and would complete as soon as possible.

My comments on this meeting
This is the one set of minutes that I have seen which clearly shows that there were very strong differences between different members of the board. More weight seems to be given to Mr Henry than to Mr Fred. In some ways that is built in to proceedings, given that Mr Henry is the general manager and Mr Fred a production manager. There is a big issue to be faced and that is how to increase income and growth. Col. Barnsley and Mr Henry seize on the idea of cutting overheads by not replacing Mr. Beeley and this simply increases Mr Fred's workload in the departments which actually need to increase output to sustain growth. On top of this he is short of a cutler. There is no way of knowing whether the meeting with Mr Wheatcroft resolved anything. The next set of minutes that I have seen, make no reference to

any of this except that Col. Barnsley had spoken to a Mr. Slack about a cutler but owing to the holidays had been unable to do anything. This decision was supposed to be acted on after the January meeting. I find it difficult to know whether this was deliberate procrastination or a lack of a sense of urgency.

I suspect these years saw the real beginning of the firm's serious decline. At this time it had about 100 employees and this number continued to decrease even after the major drop in work people when the file department closed. Competition from other parts of the world as well as a lessening of demand for specialist tools for shoemakers and leather workers took a serious toll. I also think that there was a need for greater vision at this stage of the firm's life.

Footnote. In the telephone directory for 1952 the telephone number is 21307 and in 1954 is 29263.

Chapter 9

The final years

I have been able to find only limited archive material relating to the period from the mid 1950s to the closure of the firm in 2003. The material I have seen is the minutes of some board meetings. What follows are a few facts gleaned from the memories of some of those involved.

The end of file making

When the firm was started the George Barnsley, whose drive and energy helped to build it into a thriving business, was in the file trade. He had served a full apprenticeship of seven years. Production of files was a major part of the business for over a hundred years. However in the mid 1960s Mr Henry reported at a board meeting that British filemakers were in discussion with Her Majesty's Government about the fact that they were allowing the importing of files from India. These I assume were undercutting the file producers in the United Kingdom. The importing continued.

In 1972 a discussion took place amongst the then directors about the possibility of ceasing to manufacture files. The department had made a loss for the previous 5 years. (1). Competition from both home and overseas meant that discounts were being demanded that were unsustainable. The fear was that other sales were linked to the sale of files and therefore if the department were closed files would have to be factored. This was finally and reluctantly agreed to because the firm was incurring heavy losses in this area of production. It was a difficult decision in that it involved the loss of approximately 60 jobs. For a short time the firm continued to trade in files by buying them in but in 1973 they ceased trading in all file merchandise and sold all their stocks.

The closing of the file department led to the proposal that workshops from the Globe works be moved into Cornish works in order to eliminate the amount of wasted cartage around the factory and that advertisements with a view to filling the empty space be put into the Yorkshire Post and a trade journal. Both proposals were left in abeyance. Overall the firm did make a profit of £17000 in 1971 despite the losses in specific departments.

Directors moving on

Also in the 1970s during a very depressing period, Mr Fred and his son Colin made the very difficult decision to leave the family firm and to buy a going concern across town. The 'specialism' of this new business was wood turning though they do make knives, which of course can have wooden handles, and increasingly (since the closure of George Barnsley and Sons) have made tools for leather workers.

References
(1) Minutes of the Board Meeting 19th June 1972

Part 3

Individual Stories

Chapter 1

Elizabeth Royd (nee Barnsley)

This information was extracted primarily from a book written about Attercliffe in 1932(1). Elizabeth Barnsley (1605-79) believed to be the daughter of George Barnsley of Gothard or Goddard Hall married Richard Roades, a carpenter's son who was the tenant of the mill on the Don that became known as Royds Mill from about 1637. They had one son and six daughters before Richard died. He was either unsuccessful or unfortunate in business, and when he died in 1638 his affairs were somewhat involved. His freeholds in Attercliffe had been sold, and the mill business was with difficulty retrieved from misfortune by the strenuous efforts of his widow, Elizabeth Roades, who held the mill 'at will' until 1650 when she agreed to lease the premises for twenty one years. When the lease expired in 1671 she was aged 66. After a lifetime of hard work and thirty-three years of widowhood she retired from business and built herself 'Old House at Washford Bridge'. She had her initials carved on the door and even had a decorated overmantel in the parlour bearing the date 1676 also carved with her initials (shades of Bess of Hardwick of Hardwick Hall whose initials are carved on the outside of the hall).

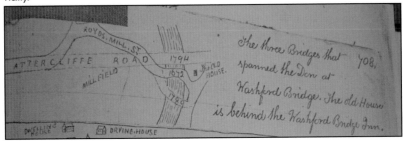

From Henry Tatton Volume 3 p.708 Sheffield Local Studies Library 942.74SQ.

It seems that this was at the time quite a busy river crossing as I understand that R.E. Leader in his lecture 'Sheffield's Old Roads' suggests that in 1607 the passage from Rotherham to Sheffield was via Washford Bridge and that the road went "by Royd's Mill to the somewhat higher level of Carlisle Street, and down Spital Hill to the Wicker." He also quotes the account of the chaplain to the Earl of Oxford who travelled from Rotherham to Sheffield in 1725 "Then, after crossing the Don twice more, the first, I think, over Washford, and the next over Lady's Bridge, we get into the town of Sheffield"(2).

According to Crossley et al (3) 'there are entries in the Arundel rentals for a corn mill and three cutlers wheels, whose tenants were successively John, Richard and the widow Rhodes…there is little doubt that this succession relates to what was to be called Royd's (Rhodes or Roades?) mill.' Ruth Roades, Elizabeth's daughter married William Fenton who became the next tenant.

This picture and those above are from www.picturesheffield.com and show the Old House with the initials of Elizabeth Roades carved above her fireplace. Her initials were also carved above the door. The bridge was known as Washford Bridge or Attercliffe Bridge. The Old House became the Fleur-de-Lys Inn but was demolished probably between 1890-1900. Note that the house when built was in a very rural setting. Don Alexander writing about the Sheffield Smelting Company whose owner John Read moved to Royds Mill in1787 describes it as then being 'a farm cum cutler's wheel cum corn mill owned by a family called Rhodes hence Royds' (4) The firm is still there under the name of Thessco and you can walk alongside it when doing the 'Five Weirs Walk'

George Barnsley was at this time renting a wheel on the Don at Wadsley. He was very possibly her relative…father, brother or cousin?

References
  (1) Vine G.R. 1932 *The Story of Old Attercliffe Sheffield,* Ward Bros pp56-59
  (2) Quoted on internet www.sheffieldhistory.co.uk/forums/index.php?showtopic=61&pid=26166&mode=threaded&start=0#entry26166
  (3) Crossley David with Jean Cass, Neville Flavell, Colin Turner 1989 *Water Power and the Sheffield Rivers*
  (4) Alexander Don, 2007 *What Made the Steel City* ALD Print p.67 Other sources consulted Shaw A.B. *The Old House near Washford Bridge Vol 2, p26 of Hunter Archaeological Magazine*, Sheffield Local History Library

Chapter 2

Tom Barnsley entertainer (1876-1918)

Tom was somewhat of a mystery man in the family. Both his brother George and half-brother Percy went into the family firm.

The brothers as boys and as young men.

Tom became a travelling entertainer. Very little is known about his career though there are some family photographs. He seems at different times to have entertained using puppets, possibly 'Punch and Judy', to have been an actor and at the end of his life to have been the manager of a theatre in Whitley Bay. The photographs indicate that much of his time was spent in the North East. We know of North and South Shields, Leeds, Scarborough and Whitley Bay.
What we know of his career can really only be told through the old photographs:

This is Tom as a young man probably taken in a photographic studio.

Mr Tom Barnsley is selling his photographs to provide gift parcels of cigarettes and tobacco to the brave men at the front.

The amount received for the photographs is acknowledged in 'The Performer' week by week

The Performer's tobacco fund is a branch of the Newspapers Patriotic Tobacco Fund registered under the War Charities Act 1916

(This information is printed on the back of the postcard)

It seems that in common with other artists Tom in order to promote his own work and to help the war effort joined in the campaign to send cigarettes and tobacco to the armed forces during WW1. The quotation below is evidence that this was common practice:

'the violinist Yazo uses his postcard to both promote himself and advertise the sale of cigarettes and, by doing so, help the War effort.

Miss Hook of Holland (2)

On the front of the picture the photographer is given as Speed Photo Co. N&S Shields

On the back of this picture is hand- written:

Tom Barnsley, Band Scene, 'Miss Hook of Holland'

Miss Hook of Holland is an English musical comedy (styled a "Dutch Musical Incident") in two acts, with music and lyrics by Paul Rubens with a book by Austen Hurgon and Reubens. The show was produced by Frank Curzon and opened at the Prince of Wales Theatre, London on the January 31, 1907, running for a very successful 462 performances. It starred Harry Grattan and Isabel Jay.

The show also had a Broadway run starring Bertram Wallis and an Australian production in 1907 and enjoyed various tours and revivals, including a 1914 revival starring Phyllis Dare. There was also a "matinee version" of the show called *Little Miss Hook of Holland*, played by children for children.

Synopsis
Mrs. Hook died young, leaving her husband with a daughter, little Sally Hook. Ludwig Schnapps, the foreman of Mr. Hook's factory, tells the story of how pretty little Miss Hook possessed a remarkable aptitude for business. By force of her character and her shrewdness, plus her invention of a wonderful liqueur called "Cream of the Sky", they make a fortune. The theft of the recipe and various complications relating to which man Sally favours and those men who would like to marry her make up the plot. The recipe finds its way back and she gets the man of her choice.

This musical comedy was extremely popular during WW1 and was performed (as an internet search reveals) all over the country by professional and amateur groups alike between the wars.

Cinderella

The American Bannister Merwin who wrote plays and was also an early filmmaker wrote 'Cinderella' which premiered sometime around 1911. This play had a character called 'Bumptious' who was a detective. To our eyes Tom's outfit hardly seems appropriate to that role but it could have been a parody of the film.

Written in the bottom right hand corner it says Tom Barnsley, 'Bumptious' in Cinderella Panto Leeds 1911-12

Australian Larrikins

This is picture taken on the 10th July 1912 when he was possibly an actor in some touring company. Handwritten on the front of the picture is:

'Manager' Australian Larrikins

This is the only picture that appears to be taken by a photographer from the South of England. Ipswich, Colchester and other places. There is no way of knowing exactly where picture was taken.

The word 'larrikin' is an Australian word of uncertain origin, meaning a rowdy person, and it was in common usage in Australia in Tom's time. Probably in those days the ties between the countries of the Empire and the Mother Country were very close and they were used to each other's colloquial terms. It is probably the same derivation as the English colloquialism 'larking about'. Unfortunately we know nothing about the play

Australian Connections

During the preparation of this book, Colin Barnsley received emails from Janet Nolan and Arthur Bentley in Australia. Arthur is now in his 90s and enjoys using the internet. It seems that whilst Janet and her cousin were doing family history research they had stumbled on the probability that Arthur was the son of Tom Barnsley. It would appear that Tom and Arthur's mother had an affair and that Tom was cited as co-respondent in her divorce proceedings. In Arthur's words:

It does seem quite strange that this family secret was not disclosed to me as an adult by my Mother, or Ernest 11 and Vera 9 years my seniors. Both the Bentley and the maternal Wilson families with their caring, forgiving but strict silence, as well as two or three other Bentley family considerations rather too lengthy to detail here, including some time lapses, would seem to absolve my mother in some way. Who knows? Whatever the circumstance I know my dear mother paid a very heavy price indeed. Thomas and my mother would have married, of that I have no doubt at all, but of course my father died before the divorce was finalized. I was born, as you know in Whitley Bay, where we lived for about three years. I was much loved by my parents, as witness the three professionally taken 'baby photos'. I have little doubt my father with his connections would have arranged for these. Also I have two memories of that time, the first: sitting on what must have been my father's lap with my hands on his as he played the piano with the black notes on a sheet of music before us. Two: some time later a hospital was mentioned by my mother, I surprised her by saying something about 'knowing what a hospital was like' and I described it 'as a row of white beds' to my mind obviously a visit to my father in hospital.

Janet wrote:
I also know looking at the puppet photograph of Tom that there is no doubt that he is my grandfather. He has a long distance between mouth and chin, but if you cover a small area and shorten the face slightly there are photographs of my father that could be interchangeable.
I think on the balance of probabilities my father is Tom's son, Given the divorce petition naming Tom, my father's money which certainly came from the Barnsleys and the fact that my grandmother's husband was so certain that my father was not his son that he filled in his army papers saying he had only 2 children. The divorce petition in which Tom was named as co-respondent mentioned that there were only two children of the marriage, my father's brother and sister. My father was born in Whitley Bay Northumberland where Tom worked, and away from Bradford, which was my grandmother's home. I know it was a family folk tale that my father was going to be called Percy, and Percy and Tom who were brothers seem to have enjoyed some sort of special relationship .It was Percy who registered Tom's death in 1918.
I know Colin expected that there would be birth certificates and the documents, which came with my father's inheritance. My grandmother wisely decided I feel to ensure that my father would be registered as a child of her marriage; it certainly saved him 92 years of being marked as illegitimate. Perhaps if she and Tom had been married he could have adopted my father.

As for the inheritance my father was simply called to the bank and handed a cheque, which came from someone named Barnsley. When he asked my grandmother whom Mr Barnsley was she said that it was someone who had known him when he was a little boy in England.

After Tom died she and her widowed sister ran a quite successful guesthouse 'Bank House' in Morecambe. My father grew up there until at age 10 he came to Australia. Unfortunately for my grandmother her former father-in-law moved from Bradford to Heysham in 1925 after his wife died, and it made it impossible for her to remain in Morecambe. Her father-in-law was very influential in the Methodist church through his temperance work and lay preaching. My grandmother's social life was much bound up with the Morecambe Methodist Church and with Heysham so close there was nothing for it but to leave.

We could never understand why she gave everything up to come to Australia there seemed to be no reason for it. I only discovered the circumstances by accident a couple of years ago. Her former father-in-law was by all accounts quite unforgiving, at odds with the rest of the family who remained quite friendly with grandma and were always most welcoming whenever she returned to England on a visit. I can only surmise that her marriage was unhappy and this was recognised by most of the people around her.

Janet, Arthur's only daughter, and her family are now Australian citizens though certainly Barnsley descendents.

Tom died at aged 42 in 1918 one of the hundreds of victims of the influenza epidemic of that year known as Spanish flu. His brother Percy was with him when he died. At the time Tom was manager of the Kursaal Theatre in Whitley Bay. This is a poster advertising a revue and confirming Tom's role as Manager:

THE KURSAAL

MARINE AVENUE.

Proprietors	...	—	...	...	...	Messrs. AMBRO and HOUGHTON
Manager	...	...	...	...	—	...	...	TOM BARNSLEY

MONDAY, JANUARY 14th, and during the Week.

ALBERT LYON presents

The Summits

Another New Revue,

"YOU CAN'T CATCH ME."

NOTE.—The Performance commences on Wednesdays, Thursdays, and Fridays at 7 p.m. Other Evenings at 7-50.

Admission—4d., 8d., and 1/3 (Reserved.)

Office Open Daily, from 1 to 5. Telephone—193, Whitley
Box Seats booked by Telephone must be claimed before performance commences.

Janet continued

I think the popular Yorkshire comedian and later film star Sydney Howard must have been at the Kursaal because my grandmother apparently had met him on several occasions and was rather knowledgeable about other theatrical and music hall people of the era. Up until now it was always a mystery to my father as to how she could possibly have known them. Her father was a commercial traveller and there were no family connections to the theatre. It's funny Dad always described the sort of puppets that Tom is demonstrating there (in the picture on Page 84) and wondering where he had seen them as a child. He always felt they were in some way connected to his family, and decided it was most likely his mother's family.

Sydney Howard mentioned above became in the 1930s a very well known film star appearing in over 20 films. In 1939 he appeared with Gracie Fields in a film called 'Clydeside Sally' which highlighted the desperate situation of the Clydeside ship builders. It concluded with Gracie singing 'Land of Hope and Glory' at the same time as a member of the Royal family launched a ship built on Clydeside. Perhaps if Tom had lived beyond his 40s he might also have gained greater renown in his chosen field.

So many sons went into family firms from choice or out of a sense of duty. The will of Tom's father Henry indicates that that was his expectation in that in the original will of 1905 his estate which included the business was divided equally between the three brothers, George, Tom and Percy. In June1907 Henry added a codicil whereby Tom was to receive an annuity of £200 a year paid quarterly instead of receiving a third of the estate. Money was to be in trust for this to happen. It seems that Tom had other ideas about how he wanted to spend his life and that by 1907 his father recognised that he was not going to enter the family business. Provision was also made for this trust money to be paid to descendents. Whether Arthur's inheritance was from Tom's savings or under the terms of Henry's will we will never know. However what seems (looking back from 2010 to the 1930s) to have been a small sum would according to the Bank of England calculator have had a purchasing power of over £20,000 today.

After Tom's untimely death a news item in a local paper about the appointment of a new manager of the theatre claims that he is well-qualified to follow in the footsteps of the late Messrs Dick Lyons and Tom Barnsley. This implies that Tom was well thought of as a manager. In the story of the family there is something unique about Tom. He had the courage to follow his creative aspirations into what in those days would have been considered a rather insecure and even dubious profession.

References
(1) http://www.ram.ac.uk/NR/rdonlyres/81F3DE18-C8F1-409F-9410-AB9000968186/0/theearlypostcard.pdf
(2) http://en.wikipedia.org/wiki/Miss_Hook_of_Holland

89

Chapter 3

Major George Barnsley (1874-1958)

George Barnsley belonged to that generation whose destiny was to see their country involved in three major wars during their lifetime. He fought in the Boer War, in WW1 he played a key role as a local recruiting officer and in WW2 it seems he was still involved with both the home guard and army cadets though in his civilian job as a manager of industry in Sheffield he would again have contributed enormous energy to organising the firm's contribution to the war effort. There can be little doubt that the army as well as the firm played a very big part in his life.

The Boer War

It took the British Army three years of fighting, three major sieges and many battles with considerable loss of life, to overwhelm the Boers (Afrikaners) and achieve a British victory. At least 25,000 Afrikaners died in the war, most of them in the concentration camps where there was an appalling lack of hygiene and medical care. This became an international outrage. The war also claimed 22,000 British and 12,000 African lives. In 1899 South Africa was an uneasy mix of states. The Transvaal and Orange Free State were both occupied by Afrikaners who were the descendants of Dutch and French settlers whilst the British colonies of Cape Colony and Natal were self-governing. The whole situation was made worse between the Boers and the British because thousands of 'Uitlanders' (foreigners, mainly English) had been drawn to the Transvaal by the gold rush. By the 1890s they were paying a considerable amount of tax and demanded equal rights. The Afrikaners refused and when the British refused a demand to stop reinforcing their troops around the Transvaal war broke out. In the end, the Afrikaners were subjected to British rule.

During the war the fighting cost many lives on both sides. During the first phase, the militarily weak British who were fighting in a hostile country over difficult terrain with long lines of communications and inappropriate tactics were primarily on the defensive. The Boers attacked on two fronts: into Natal from the Transvaal and into the Northern Cape from the Orange Free State. During one week (sometimes called Black week 10-15 December 1899) the Boers defeated the British in a number of major skirmishes and besieged the important towns of Ladysmith, Mafeking and Kimberley.

Eventually large numbers of British reinforcements were landed, and slowly the war turned in Britain's favour. The British, under Lord Kitchener and Frederick Sleigh Roberts, 1st Earl Roberts, relieved the besieged towns, beat the Boers in the field, and took Bloemfontein in February 1900, followed by Johannesburg and Pretoria in May and June. However at the end of 1900 the war entered its most destructive phase. For fifteen months Boer commandos attacked British bases and Kitchener responded with a scorched-earth policy.

Farms belonging to both Boers and Africans were destroyed and the Boer inhabitants of the countryside were rounded up and held in the concentration camps.

The commandos continued their attacks many of them deep into the Cape Colony and General Jan Smuts lead his forces to within 50 miles of Cape Town. However Kitchener's drastic and brutal methods slowly led to British success. The Boers had unsuccessfully sued for peace in March 1901 but finally accepted the loss of their independence by signing the Peace of Vereeniging.

There is a series of crime fiction novels by John Malcolm featuring an art expert called Tim Simpson who manages what is known as the art fund for a small private investment bank. His adventures occur as he hunts for new pictures or antiques for this fund. In *Circles and Squares* Tim Simpson visits an old South African friend called Darkie Collins:

On my left a long wall extending to the stairs was darkened by a big oak-framed steel engraving of Buller's troops crossing the Tugela, all horses, gun carriages and pith helmets by Carton Woodville or Paget or one of those…'you mean you've built up this library of images over a period and now it brings you income' The Boer war's got much more material, photography was really taking off then…(1) This reference indicates the Edwardians and later generations came to see the Boer war as an exciting period for collectors. It seems that George Barnsley was one of those early photographers and whilst in Africa he took several photographs of sites that were already well-known as well as pictures of the unit's journey. Later he took photographs in Sheffield's Corn Exchange which was his headquarters in WW1. This is a unique collection of pictures.

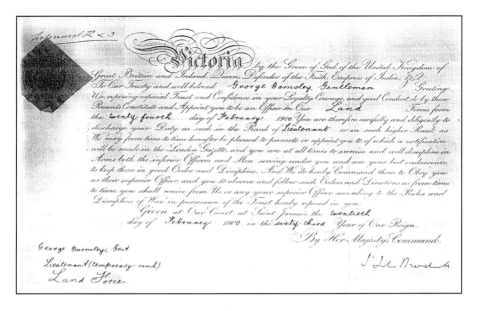

George was appointed as a second lieutenant in the first West Riding Royal Engineers (Volunteers) on the 13th October 1896 and promoted to Lieutenant (temporary rank), Land Forces on the 20th February 1900. He and 25 men sailed from Southampton on March 10th 1900 in the *Tintagel Castle*

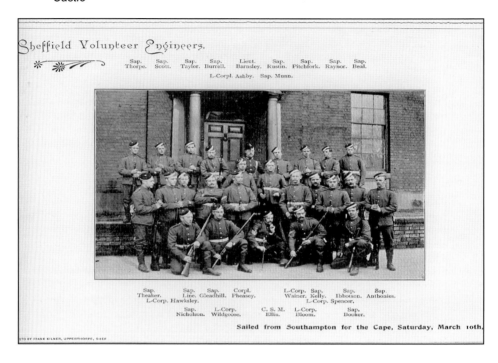

Sheffield Volunteer Engineers.

Sap. Thorpe. Sap. Scott. Sap. Taylor. Sap. Burrell. Lieut. Barnsley. Sap. Rustin. Sap. Pitchfork. Sap. Raynor. Sap. Beal.

L-Corpl. Ashby. Sap. Munn.

Sap. Thealker. Sap. Line. L-Corp. Hawksley. Sap. Gleadhill. Corpl. Pheasey. L-Corp. Wainer. Sap. Kelly. L-Corp. Spencer. Sap. Ibbotson. Sap. Anthonies.

Sap. Nicholson. L-Corp. Wildgoose. C. S. M. Ellis. L-Corp. Bloom. Sap. Booker.

Sailed from Southampton for the Cape, Saturday, March 10th,

PHOTO BY FRANK KILNER, UPPERTHORPE, SHEF.

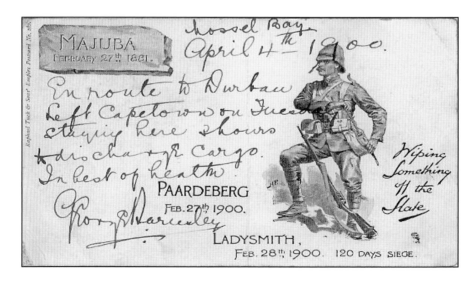

92

The postcard on the previous page was presumably posted not long after his arrival in South Africa. The British were resoundingly defeated at Majuba Hill during the first Boer War hence the caption 'wiping something off the slate'. Mossel Bay where it seems that some cargo was unloaded, is about half way between Cape Town and Port Elizabeth. Since he says that he was en route for Durban it seems likely that the ship continued its voyage round the Cape and that the engineers disembarked at Durban. From there they went to join the 17th Field Company of the Royal Engineers at Pietermaritzburg leaving there on April 10th to join the second division at the front under General Clery at Elandslaagte. This was prior to the advance of General Buller through North Natal. Their work consisted of improving the defences at Ladysmith and general duties with water supply. This is an extract from www.angloboerwar.com. It is not specifically about George Barnsley's unit though we know for certain they worked on bridges and railway as a part of the 17th Field Company and amongst his photographs are pictures of the Tugela River and the area around Ladysmith. It gives a picture of what the Company must have experienced.

17th Field Company at Durban. It was engaged on the Tugela, and suffered in conducting its operations under fire. Nowhere in South Africa have the Engineers done better service than in the operations in and about Ladysmith. They have been continually employed in assisting the gunners by preparing the positions to be taken up, and in the digging of shelter trenches, besides all the work, which has fallen to them at the camps. At Frere they built a bridge alongside that which the Boers had so thoroughly wrecked, and they found a great deal of work in repairing the railway line.

Majuba Hill shown on his postcard home was where the British suffered a major defeat during the first Boer war in February 1881. The forces were inadequately equipped and General Colley died there. Victorian England tended to view Generals killed in action as martyrs. The Battle of Paadeburg was also a British disaster. The postcard was perhaps issued to the troops as a means of motivating them and the recipients back home.

George Barnsley's war can be seen through the series of photographs that he took himself during in his time in South Africa. These cover a variety of subjects and include photographs of some of his fellow officers as well as the men. The pictures selected show identifiable places that are well-known landmarks of the Boer war, though there are also pictures of subjects like Boer shelters, a goldmine and a prospector 'O'Neill of Mount Prospect'. All of the pictures give an impression of stones, dust and dryness and all the work looks very hard going.

The Volunteer Engineers were employed in setting up or restoring lines of communication in tasks that involved building, bridging, telegraph, electrical and railway work. George's pictures as far as location can be identified are in the area of Northern Natal. Places that get a mention are the Tugela Bridge which was a crossing over one of the widest rivers in the region. The original bridge was 200 yards long and was destroyed and replaced with a pontoon bridge. I think it is possible this was a picture taken en route rather

93

than showing a piece of work on which he and his men had been engaged. To give a very rough idea of distances Durban to Newcastle (S.Africa) would be the approximate equivalent of London to York in the British Isles (about 200 miles) and Newcastle (S.Africa) to Standerton would be about as far as York to Morpeth in the British Isles. (100 miles). Ladysmith where he took pictures of the 'Big Tom' gun site was about as far as Nottingham from London (120 miles).

It is recorded in a magazine extract (dated Nov 7th 1903 but magazine not named) found in the family papers that the company took part in the general advance and went by Helpmakaar ridge, Dundee, Dannhauser and Newcastle where they did extensive railway repairs. On April 29th they marched to Ingogo taking up the front facing Laing's Nek repairing the railways as they went. The extract below gives some idea of the terrain through which this group of Sheffield volunteer engineers trekked. The two on page 96 taken by George Barnsley show the entrance to the Laing's Nec tunnel and his men working to clear the line into the tunnel.

> *"The mountains which on the edge of Basutoland rise to a height of ten thousand feet," writes Mr. Bryce, "break down toward Natal in tremendous precipices. Near Ladysmith the frontier of the Orange Free State coincides with a high watershed, crossed by only a few passes."[2] Where this boundary between Natal and the Free State ends, that of the Transvaal begins, and soon after turns sharply to the southward, the new direction forming with the old a very acute angle, with apex to the north. Here, just within the territory of Natal, is Majuba Hill, whose name has been in the mouths of all men, and Laing's Nek, less familiarly known. The narrow neck of rugged country embraced between the legs of this angle is about sixty miles long, from Majuba to Glencoe. Recent events have familiarised to us many of the names along this line of rail — Glencoe, Dundee (the terminus of a short branch), Colenso, Estcourt, and Ladysmith itself; while the winding character of the track, as mapped, compared with the Free State road sufficiently indicates the character of the country in which obstacles have to be circumvented as well as overcome. The grade is in places as high as one in thirty, though that is being reduced; but one in forty is common. Pietermaritzburg, the capital, fifty miles from Durban in a straight line, is 2,200 feet above the sea. Three hundred miles from its starting-point the road reaches an elevation of over five thousand feet, at Laing's Nek, through which it passes by a tunnel. (www.angloboerwar.com)*

This map that I have constructed, shows the approximate position of places named in photographs taken by George Barnsley or mentioned in correspondence. The scale is approximately 60 English miles to 1 inch. They disembarked at Durban on South Africa's east coast and finished at Standerton about a hundred miles south of Johannesburg so the assumption is that they took a northwesterly route. The photographs could have been taken on the outward or homeward march or both.

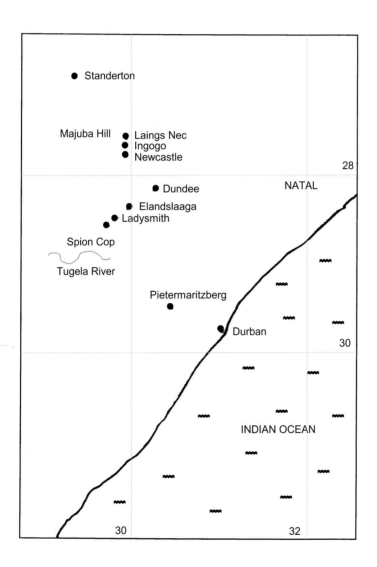

Tugela Bridge Natal

During the siege of Ladysmith the Boers used a big Cannon against the British that was known as Big Tom. One of George's photographs shows the place where this gun was situated. He labels it 'Big Tom emplacement Mubalwana Ladysmith'. (Picture below)

After finishing the work on the tunnel, they marched on towards Standerton in the Transvaal where they found 17 locomotives in a broken-down state. They were handed over to George and his men 'who speedily put them into working order'.

The picture below George describes as 'the first engine at Standerton'. There are other pictures showing work being done to restore railway lines. This was an engine on which George probably worked. (See letter on Page 99 from Major F. M. Clubb).

The two pictures below are labelled 'Standerton Kop 4.7 gun' and 'Boer war entanglement outside Ladysmith'

Standerton Kop 4.7 gun

Boer war entanglement outside Ladysmith

Towards the end of the fifty or more pictures that George Barnsley took is this one of Majuba Hill below:

The *Sheffield Daily Telegraph* published a letter on the 25th January 1901 from Major F. M. Clubb, officer commanding 17th Field Company R.E. in Standerton to Colonel Bingham. This is an extract:

'The section of non-commissioned officers and men under Lieut.G.Barnsley joined my company at Elandslaagte, Natal in April and left on their way home in October 1900, from this place.

As soon as they joined the company I made them No. 4 section of the 17th Company, R.E. under their own officer and as such they remained until their departure, taking their share of the work until they left us, exactly as any other section of the company without any distinction whatever.

First let me say that their conduct and discipline were admirable...

The men were all round much younger than the sappers of the 17th company and not so used to really hard pick and shovel work; and I think at first they found the pay and real work very hard indeed but they were admirably handled by Lieutenant Barnsley and in this respect they improved very much. In fact I think I may say that they joined us as boys and returned to you as men. Their spirit was excellent all through: I was a little afraid at first that the hard work and the long marches during the advance by Helpmakaar through the Biggarsberg would be too much for them but I never heard a word of grumbling from first to last.

The excellent spirit that animated the section I attribute very largely to Lieutenant Barnsley, and also to Sergeant Ellis and Corporal Pheasy both excellent non-commissioned officers. Lieutenant Barnsley is an officer I should be proud to have under me at any time. He is extremely hardworking and conscientious and had a great control and influence over his men. He was most good-tempered and tactful and always willing to do any work that was wanted at any time. He was always in touch with his men, and their excellent behaviour, I am sure, was largely due to his personal influence and example. He also did most useful work for me apart from his section many times; his knowledge of machinery was especially valuable. He overhauled numbers of pumping engines on the railway line and he put in working order the railway locomotives that we found in Standerton on our arrival and had them running before the arrival of the N.U. Railway staff at the station. His personal services to me were invaluable in every way, and I hope that I may count him as a personal friend.'

After doing general duties including water supply, road-making and blockhouses and patrolling the line north and south of Standerton, they received orders on October 10th to return home. They sailed on November 1st in the *Avon Castle* arriving on November 26th and in Sheffield on the 29th where they got a very warm reception. A plaque in the Town Hall gave recognition to all those from Sheffield including the Volunteer Engineers who served in the Boer war. This can be found at the top of the first flight of steps leading into the town hall on the left wall. There is a photograph on the next page together with a detail showing George Barnsley's name at the bottom of the first column in the picture. Also illustrated is his invitation card to the event at the town hall recognising the services of the volunteer engineers.

No.	Rank	Name		No.	Rank	Name
32396	PTE.	MIDDLETON A.			LIEUT.	O'SHEA L. T.
32409	,,	NORCLIFFE J. H.		5915	SGT.	ELLIS H. C.
32410	,,	OLDFIELD W.		5916	CPL.	PHEASEY E.
32421	SGT.	PRESSLEY H.		5917	,,	WAINER J. W.
32445	PTE.	SEAMAN W.		5918	LC. CPL.	BLOOM E.
32451	,,	SHEPHERD W.		5919	SPR.	ASHBY J.
32485	,,	WORSLEY C. W.		5921	,,	BOOKER W.
37785	,,	WEBB J.		5922	,,	BEAL T. S.
38294	,,	BARTON W.		5923	,,	BURRELL W. E.
38299	,,	CASTLE H.		5924	,,	GLEADHILL J. R.
38301	,,	CHAPPELL T.		5925	,,	HAWKSLEY E. L.
38305	,,	CROOKES J.		5927	,,	KELLEY W.
38327	,,	MANN R.		5928	,,	LINE H.
38330	,,	MORTON C.		5929	,,	MUNN J.
39481	,,	SEMMENS A.		5930	,,	NICHOLSON C.
39511	,,	KELLINGTON J. W.		5931	,,	PITCHFORK W.
39524	,,	STUBBING B.		5932	,,	RAYNOR J.
40036	,,	EMMERSON E.		5933	,,	RASTIN G. H.
40040	,,	HARRISON J. W.		5934	,,	SPENCER W.
40042	,,	NASEBY T. W.		5935	,,	SCOTT F.
41592	,,	JOYCE W.		5936	,,	TAYLOR W.
42430	,,	STEVENSON J. R.		5937	,,	THEAKER A.
42436	,,	MASON J.		5938	,,	THORPE J.
42443	,,	HUNTER R.		5939	,,	WILDGOOSE J.
43102	,,	LOCKWOOD J. T.		8225	SGT.	HUME G. A.
43111	,,	BUTLER G. A.		8226	CPL.	IBBOTSON E.
43113	,,	ATKIN W.		8227	,,	ANTHONIES H.
43116	,,	WALSH J.		8228	LC. CPL.	TAYLOR F.
43118	,,	LOCKWOOD H.		8229	SPR.	ASTWOOD W.
43122	CPL.	BOOKER F.		8230	,,	BURNAND C.
43127	PTE.	HULMES F.		8231	,,	TORR H.
43589	,,	BROWN J. H.		8232	,,	CARNALL H.
43594	,,	CROOKES H.		8233	,,	CADDICK S. R.
43607	,,	JOHNSON J.		8234	,,	ELLIS J.
43622	,,	WHYMAN M.		8235	,,	EDWARDS G.
				8236	,,	FROGGATT J.
				8237	,,	HARRISON S.
				8238	,,	HETHERINGTON H.
				8239	,,	HOLMES S.
				8240	,,	LIGHTFOOT G.

1st WEST YORK
ROYAL ENGINEERS
(VOLUNTEERS)

LIEUT. BARNSLEY G.

CITY OF SHEFFIELD.

RECOGNITION OF SERVICES OF VOLUNTEERS IN THE SOUTH AFRICAN WAR.

THE LORD MAYOR AND LADY MAYORESS

(ALDERMAN AND MRS. J. WYCLIFFE WILSON)

request the pleasure of the company of

Lieut. G. Barnsley

At the TOWN HALL, SHEFFIELD, on

WEDNESDAY, APRIL 8th, 1903, from 8 to 11 p.m.,

On the occasion of the unveiling of the Tablet in the front entrance of the Town Hall, on which are inscribed the names of the Volunteers, Ambulance Men and Telegraphists of Sheffield who volunteered and went out on active service with the British Army in South Africa.

The presentation to the Volunteers, etc., of Photogravures of the Tablet will take place in the Reception Room immediately after the unveiling.

LIGHT REFRESHMENTS.

THIS CARD SHOULD BE PRODUCED AT THE TOWN HALL TO SECURE ADMISSION.

There can be no doubt that the Boer war, however viewed by the Victorians, was a war that failed to show the British in a favourable light and was strategically either disastrous or exceedingly cruel. As was often the case it was mostly the foot soldiers and junior officers who paid with their lives and men like George Barnsley must have had extremely hard conditions in which to work on these projects intended to provide communications and supply lines to the fighting men. What they achieved was remarkable.

> 'It would be difficult to conceive of a campaign in which the work of the Engineers would be more arduous than it was in South Africa, or in which the difference between middling and excellent service on their part would be more acutely felt by those in command or by the body of the fighting troops. The corps is fortunate in that in no quarter, official or unofficial, has there been the slightest attempt to bestow on them anything but the heartiest commendations. All the generals appreciated the difficulties they had to contend with and overcame. It has often been remarked that the natural courage required to prevent men running away from a shower of shrapnel or a hail of rifle-bullets, where the men have the power of returning the storm even in diminished force, is a totally different quality from the trained, inculcated heroism which enables men to go out in the face of certain extreme danger to repair a telegraph line, examine a bit of railway, or build a bridge without the excitement afforded by the opportunity of returning fire. The Engineers had to do all these things and a hundred others. The splendid conduct of Major Irvine's pontoon company in "constructing well and rapidly, under fire", the bridges required on the Tugela, was said by General Buller "to deserve much praise"; and unofficial writers were wonder-struck at the cool, methodical work, flurry, haste, or anything slipshod being unseen. Every plank set in its place, every knot tied as if at a drill. (Extract from the website www.angloboerwar.com)'

Arrival in Sheffield

When the volunteers arrived back in Sheffield on November 29th 1900 they were greeted by the Lord Mayor and received a tumultuous welcome from the general public. The *Sheffield Independent* described it as 'scenes of unparalleled enthusiasm'. It was thought that the war was nearly over but in fact it was 1902 before the Boer commanders reluctantly accepted the British terms. The whole unit returned unscathed. A cartoon appeared in the local paper together with the text beside the picture. (See page 102)

OUR FANCY PORTRAIT GALLERY.—NO. 58

THE HERO OF THE HOUR

Lieutenant Barnsley, who is a young member of a well-known Sheffield family looked a fine figure on horseback when he returned home at the head of his gallant little band of Engineer volunteers from the war-'the hero of the hour'. He and his men had a great popular reception from the thousands of citizens who lined the streets, in recognition of their services for Queen and country in South Africa. As an officer his military duties have made him a fine soldier, crisp in utterance, alert and stalwart. He sailed from Southampton on March 10th and saw service with his men in a warm corner of Natal and in other parts of the battlefield. His experience of practical warfare should be of great value to the Sheffield Engineer volunteers. His safe return home to become' the hero of the hour' must have pleased him, as it delighted all patriotic citizens.

In early December the unit attended a service at Ranmoor Church where they had been just ten months previously before they left for South Africa. The following information is from the *Sheffield Daily Telegraph* of Dec. 3rd 1900. They assembled at their headquarters in Glossop Rd. The route lined with onlookers took them from there to the church along Clarkson Road and up Endcliffe Vale Road. Police managed the crowd and the parade was led by two bands and immediately behind them 'Lieutenant Barnsley and his khaki comrades'. Behind them there were two or three Indian Mutiny veterans and then 370 members of the corps. In his sermon the vicar expressed sentiments which we very much associate with the Victorian era.

'Every part of our vast empire was aroused and her sons responded to the call of duty. From every part they turned to the old Mother country in a spirit of splendid patriotism and heartfelt devotion. In the dark hour England and her Colonies were found to be one and the readiness with which all responded to the call to arms proved that our biggest and best national qualities were still what they were in the days of our fathers…It was not merely a question of upholding our military prestige but we all at that time realised only too truly that the very existence or our vast Empire, its integrity and its glory depended on the ultimate victory of the British arms.'

When after the service they returned to the Drill Hall Mr C. W. Kaysor of Endcliffe Grange presented each man with £5 as an expression of his gratitude for their willingness to serve Queen and country.

The lieutenant's return to the works of George Barnsley and Sons was equally celebrated. On the next page is the report from the *Sheffield Daily Telegraph* December 3rd 1900:

LIEUT. BARNSLEY AND HIS WORKMEN.

The workpeople of George Barnsley and Sons, of Cornish Street, of which firm Lieutenant Barnsley is a member, prepared a very hearty welcome for him on his return from the front. The works were decorated with a completeness which has probably never been excelled. The firm provides employment for about 360 persons, and all joined heartily in a scheme for adorning the workshops in a way which should be evidence at once of patriotism and of the kindly feeling which exists between employer and employed. The result was that every one of the numerous shops was made bright with bannerettes and mottoes of welcome. In one of the file warehouses, the women surrounded a doorway with pictures of popular heroes and of war scenes, all draped with red, white, and blue bunting, and strings of small flags were hung across the room, the whole effect being very attractive. The large machine file-cutting shop looked very well. No elaborate designs were worked out, and no costly materials were used, but wherever one looked the combination of red, white, and blue was noticeable, either in the form of paper bannerettes stretching in lines from wall to wall, or of bands encircling the pillars, and in many places were hung Japanese lanterns. At the entrance of the shoe-knife forging shop, was a steel plate with the words " God Save the Queen " inscribed on it, and mottoes such as ". A hearty welcome to you," and " For Auld Lang Syne," were prominent everywhere. In the hammer forging shop a " charger " was rigged up as a cannon, described as Long Tom. In every shop almost every inch of space was filled with paper bannerettes—forgers, polishers, warehouse women; and all were inspired in their work by the colours of the Union Jack. The work of decorating began last Tuesday, and it considerably interfered with the work of earning money for the rest of the week. There was a half-holiday on Thursday, in order that the workpeople might see the Engineers arrive, and on Friday, when Lieutenant Barnsley visited the works, all the employes received him with great enthusiasm, and many accompanied him on his tour of inspection. The popular officer shook hands with everyone in the employ of the firm, and great good-feeling was manifested on both sides. Hundreds of people went round the works to see the decorations on Friday and Saturday.

His Personal Life

By the time he returned from the Boer War he was about 26 years old and still unmarried. It is a bit of a mystery as to how he met his wife. She was actually a guest in his father's house on the night of the census on March 31st 1901. Her name was Mabel Gittus and the census states that she was born in Mildenhall, Suffolk. She still lived in Suffolk as the marriage took place there in the summer of 1905 when George was about thirty one years old and Mabel two years younger. How did they meet? We can never know for certain but I do speculate as to whether it was to do with a business trip. Her family were farmers on quite a big scale. Her grandfather Robert Gittus in 1861 employed 28 men and 18 boys. A farm employing this number must have had horses, so did Robert and later his son Fredrick, Mabel's father buy tools for harness leather workers and possibly other agricultural tools from George Barnsley and Sons? The picture below shows a fairly well-to-do wedding, the picture was probably taken at the bride's family home.

There is a family story that she decided she wanted to marry him when she was only sixteen years old. After the marriage the couple settled in Sheffield so that George could continue his management responsibilities as part of the family firm, though also he continued to maintain his responsibilities as an officer with the volunteers.

In due course they had four children: George, Fred, Edward and Elizabeth. Edward died in a motorbike accident as a very young man. A motorist who had pulled out of a side road hit him. George and Fred went into the family firm. This picture is of George and Mabel with Fred (left) Elizabeth and George and dates to the period after WW1 but before WW2.

The Barnsleys lived in Victoria Rd and later in Collegiate Crescent, Sheffield.

The First World War

When war broke out George was ready to get involved. He was 40 years old and received a letter on the 24th September 1914 that appears to have been sent to all ex-officers whose names were on the register of the National Reserves. It was to ask who would be willing to serve should the War Office require their services. George duly completed the requisite form. There are several telegrams in the family archives concerning his going for an interview in York. At the time he was staying probably on the firm's business at the Waverley Hotel in Edinburgh. The form specifically asked in Question 5 *whether medically fit to serve at home*? He answered in the affirmative. In response to the questions about special qualifications and nature of employment he emphasised that he spoke fluent German that he had learnt abroad and fairly fluent French not learnt abroad.

He felt that if a prisoner-of-war camp was set up near Sheffield or indeed elsewhere he had all the right qualifications to become the commanding officer. These qualifications included not only his language skills but also his experience as a manager of men not only in the Boer War but also at the works where he had 400 employees. He also had experience as a Royal Engineers Divisional Officer in managing camps and buildings. He did feel he would need a promotion to give him formal authority. He filled in forms and wrote letters and went for various interviews and had support from others but was unsuccessful in acquiring such a post. It seems from the correspondence that this was a bitter disappointment.

There are also letters of refusal from the Tyneside Commercial Battalion and the Anti-Aircraft Corps. His first appointment was as assistant recruiting officer to Major Goodyear and then to Major Firth. George was in charge of the Registration Department. He eventually succeeded Major Firth as officer commanding the Sheffield Recruiting Area and was promoted to the rank of captain. This was in June 1916. At this time the army was dependent on volunteers. There was no conscription. It seems that George had many qualities, which fitted him for the post, but as Arthur Balfour of Donnemorra Steelworks said in a letter of congratulations, George was able 'to view things not only from a military point of view, but also from a manufacturing point of view'. In a city like Sheffield where steel production and the manufacture of armaments was so crucial to the war effort, this perspective would have given George the capacity to make informed decisions. Letters of congratulations that survive come from the owners and directors of what were then major industrial concerns. These were personal and in one instance handwritten and sent from other industrialists who obviously knew him personally. Note the details such as information about the Ashton nephew in the letter at the bottom of the next page. A handwritten letter from W.A.Macdonald of Wicker Iron Works both congratulated and thanked him 'for the kindness shown to me when on firm's business'. There is also a quite lengthy handwritten letter of congratulations from the major who commanded the administrative centre at Wakefield. He says '*I am delighted to think that at last you have received the recognition that you deserved.*' The *Sheffield Daily Telegraph* said on May 11th 1916 that '*His promotion it may be presumed, is attributable to the energy and enthusiasm he has displayed in this important and responsible work. All who have been brought into association with the popular officer will be glad to know that his well-merited promotion will not involve his removal from Sheffield.*'

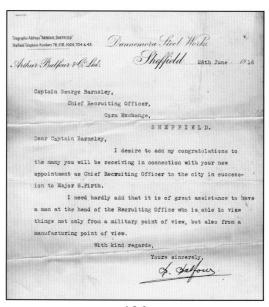

CYCLOPS·STEEL·&·IRON·WORKS.

SHEFFIELD.

28th. June 1916.

Dear Captain Barnsley,

      The only moment I had to spare to look at this morning's paper revealed the happy incident of your appointment as Senior Recruiting Officer of Sheffield.

      I believe you are almost tired of seeing Cammells at your office, so I wish to tender to you my heartiest congratulations by letter.

              Yours faithfully,

FOR AND ON BEHALF OF
CAMMELL LAIRD & Co., LIMITED.

Director & Secretary.

Captain G. Barnsley,

    Corn Exchange,

        Sheffield.

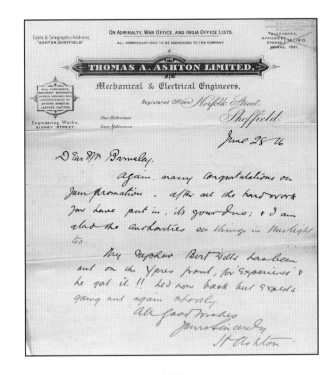

ON ADMIRALTY, WAR OFFICE, AND INDIA OFFICE LISTS.

Cable & Telegraphic Address,
"ASHTON, SHEFFIELD."

ALL COMMUNICATIONS TO BE ADDRESSED TO THE COMPANY.

TELEPHONES,
OFFICES
STORES
WORKS, 1561.

THOMAS A. ASHTON LIMITED.

Mechanical & Electrical Engineers,

MILL FURNISHERS,
MACHINERY MERCHANTS
STORES CONTRACTORS
MANUFACTURERS OF
DRIVING BANDS &c.
LEATHER FACTORS

Engineering Works,
SIDNEY STREET.

Registered Offices Norfolk Street
Sheffield.

Our Reference
Your Reference

June 28 '16

Dear Mr Barnsley,

    Again, many congratulations on your promotion - after all the hard work you have put in, it's your due; & I am glad the authorities see things in this light too.

    My nephew Bert Wills has been out on the Ypres front, for experience & he got it !! He's now back but expects going out again shortly.

    All good wishes

    Yours sincerely,

    N Ashton

Other letters of congratulations came from William E. Hart who was the Sheffield Town Clerk and B.W. Winder of the Continental Steel Works Sheffield.

The telegram below was sent to recruiting offices on the 4th August 1914. On the back is handwritten by person unknown '1914-1918 Mobilization of reservists Northern Command, York'.

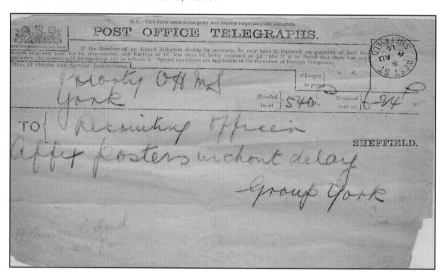

This is a photograph of a recruiting poster from the family archives.

The recruiting office was based in the Corn Exchange in Exchange Street. It was a large building and an album of photographs exists showing staff at work in the various parts of the building. To modern eyes the conditions look very austere. The four pictures on the next page show the building itself, as well as an internal view of some of the people who did the administrative work that was involved in the recruiting process. There is also a group picture taken in1916 which may have been taken to mark the end of Major Firth's command. Other pictures in the collection show staff and 'offices' and one photograph is of rather primitive cubicles and an even more primitive radiator stove. I assume this was the area where medical examinations were held.

109

There were just over a hundred civilian staff employed in the Exchange, most of them women.

I think that one of George's colleagues with whom he formed a close working relationship was William Lapper who in July 1916 was the Colonel commanding No 5 district. There are seven letters altogether from this man to George and they are all handwritten and share a lot of thought and opinion which is what leads me to believe that they knew one another well and that William Lapper had great respect for George. All were written in the summer of 1916.

The first one congratulates George on his appointment as the man in charge of the recruiting office and also on his promotion to Captain. In early July, Colonel Lapper's letter thanks him for the photograph. He writes '*I shall always value this photograph as a memory of a band of grand workers whose united efforts and camaraderie have done so much for the cause of their country.*

To one who rather shivers at the remembrance of the Corn Exchange of December 1915 the Corn Exchange of July 1916 is more than a comforter. I consider that really when you are working for England it is out of place in me to tender you any personal thanks but I think I may be allowed to express to you all my gratitude for your very great share in lightening my entire responsibilities'.

A letter in mid July asks for a diagram of the organisation of 'your office' showing the departments and status and nature of staff employed. It almost seems as though the writer wanted this as a model. About two weeks later he is urging George: *We must get men…I hope that you will do everything you can …to get Military Representatives to stiffen their backs and appeal against the decisions of local tribunals…without men we shall have no England'*. In June 1916 the Military Service Act had been passed which introduced conscription for all men between 19 and 41. It was possible by appealing to a local tribunal to get a certificate of exemption that covered such things as: engaged in other work in the national interest, serious hardship which could be financial, business or personal, ill health, and conscientious objection. In South Yorkshire there were probably many men working in the heavy metal trades who would be exempt from military service by virtue of their job and William Lapper does acknowledge this. . George replied though we have no record of what he said. Within a day or two back came William's response *'Women can do much but like others have their limits'*. However he is still urging George to find more men. In August he lets George know of some organisational changes and tells him that he has made representation that George because he is in charge of an area should be promoted to major.

It was almost another year before the promotion came and with it the letters of congratulations from the leaders of the business community. Typical of these is a letter from Leonard Colley, a Sheffield firm of Leather Merchants and Factors. Other letters came from Walter Tyzack of Broom Hall, T.E.Venables Secretary to the Board of Joseph Jonas, Colver & Co. Limited, Continental & Novo Steel Works, from Arthur Balfour and Co of the Dannemora Steel Works. Mr Walker (Wing and Son accountants) had been a member of staff at the recruiting office when George Barnsley had joined it. He wrote *'as one...(who) had been for some little while under your command, I can without undue flattery say that the promotion has been earned by sheer merit'*. In addition there is a letter of congratulation from Major Firth who was his predecessor in charge at the Sheffield Recruiting Office and who writes from a Scarborough address. He includes the comment: *'I suppose that Mr Allen would have told you of our experience of one of our airships and an enemy submarine. They both created a little excitement.'* This is one example of the letters of congratulation. The firm of Colley and Sons were no doubt customers of the firm of George Barnsley and Sons whose speciality was tools for leather workers.

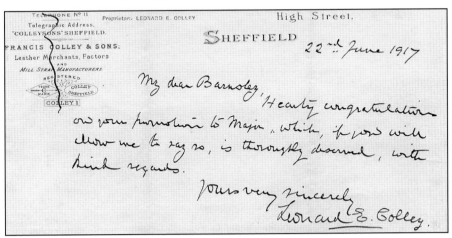

The promotion to major followed an inspection in the autumn of 1916. The report is in the family archives and everything at the very least was ticked as satisfactory. The range in the report is from 'satisfactory' to 'very good'. It does reveal that there were 14 male and 92 female staff employed at the time. There were also 12 military representatives. The General Remarks are of greatest interest (see next page). The suggestion seems to be that they were doing a great job though understaffed and that some procedures outside the senior recruiting officer's control were not particularly helpful to the work.

There is a small local newspaper article in the family archives that is dated Nov. 19th 1918 which reports that Major Barnsley 'is leaving this city to take up an appointment as regional officer for civil national service at Leeds'. The article also comments that *'Major Barnsley has been full of his enthusiasm for his work at Sheffield; his grasp of the great mass of detail has been remarkable and he has built up an organisation which has been a credit to him and to all those closely associated with him.'* I suspect that this move never actually happened as the war came to an end on November 11th 1918. There is no other family archive material relating to it.

The greatest accolade that George received in recognition of his war work was the Order of the British Empire which was presented to him at Buckingham Palace by George V on September 24th 1918. The family archives contain the cutting from *The Times* (September 25th 1918), the section known as '*Court Circular*' in which his name is recorded. He was required to attend the Palace in 'service dress' and to be there by 10am, the investiture being at 10.30.

George R. I.

George the Fifth by the Grace of God of the United Kingdom of Great Britain and Ireland, and of the British Dominions beyond the Seas King Defender of the Faith, Emperor of India and Sovereign of the Most Excellent Order of the British Empire to Our trusty and well beloved George Barnsley Esquire Temporary Major in Our Army **Greeting** whereas We have thought fit to nominate and appoint you to be an Officer of Our said Most Excellent Order of the British Empire, We do by these presents grant unto you the Dignity

of an Officer of Our said Order and hereby authorise you to have hold and enjoy the said Dignity and Rank of an Officer of Our aforesaid Order together with all and singular the privileges thereunto belonging or appertaining.

Given at Our Court at Saint James's under Our Sign Manual and Seal of Our said Order, this Third day of June 1918, in the Ninth year of Our Reign

By the Sovereign's Command.

Edward P

Grand Master

Grant of the dignity of an Officer of the Most Excellent Order of the British Empire to Temporary Major George Barnsley

GENERAL REMARKS.

RECRUITING MACHINERY AND EFFICIENCY OF STAFF.

The Recruiting Machinery is in very efficient condition and is well organised.

Staff is very efficient and is working well, but for an office which has nearly 100,000 names on the Register two Officers are insufficient for any adequate supervision; two more Officers are required.

The present lady supervising clerks are doing exceedingly well but have more responsibility thrust upon them than is desirable or fair to them.   Captain Barnsley has done great work and is recommended for promotion.

TRIBUNALS.

All reported satisfactory.

ADVISORY COMMITTEES AND MILITARY REPRESENTATIVES.

All reported satisfactory.

MINISTRY OF MUNITIONS and DEBADGING.

The present system whereby the Ministry's Debadging Department intimate the number of men that are to be badged in any particular firm, but do not state the names, is futile from the Recruiting Officer's point of view.

SUBSTITUTION.

Most of the men who are "Substitutable" by reason of their Medical Category are reported to be either in certified occupations, or in employment on account of which Tribunals will grant exemption.

DERBY,   (SD) H.H.Burney, Brig-General
11.10.16.   Inspector of Recruiting.

There is no doubt that in the years following WW1 George maintained involvement with the reservists of the British Army but my guess is that most of his energy went into working with the family firm.

The Second World War

We know very little of George's army involvement in WW2. However one document survives in the family archives which gives some useful information. This is a programme for a 'Grand Concert' to be held on December 12th 1940. It was organised by Sheffield Home Guard 5th Battalion 'E' Company by kind permission of Major George Barnsley who was to be present at the concert. The programme is reproduced below. What I find most poignant is the item in small print at the bottom of the page listing the items:

'In the event of an air raid warning, patrons who wish to leave the hall are requested to do so quietly. The nearest shelters are situate at the library, Surrey Street and Woodhouse's Fargate. The show will continue. Thank you'.

113

I doubt the show continued as December 12th was in fact the worst night of the Sheffield Blitz. Given that it was suggested that people wanting to make use of shelters would find the nearest in Surrey St or Fargate means that the concert must have been somewhere like the Victoria Hall or the Montgomery Hall. Bombs fell all round this area and I suspect that this may have been one occasion when the show did not go on. It was a night when many civilians lost their lives.

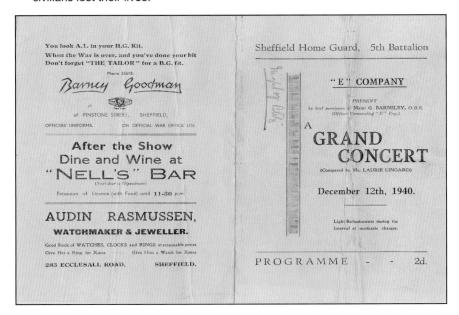

You look A.1. in your H.G. Kit.
When the War is over, and you've done your bit
Don't forget "THE TAILOR" for a B.G. fit.

Phone 25618.

Barney Goodman

of PINSTONE STREET, SHEFFIELD.

OFFICERS' UNIFORMS.   ON OFFICIAL WAR OFFICE LIST.

After the Show
Dine and Wine at
"NELL'S" BAR
(Next door to Hippodrome)

Extension of Licence (with Food) until 11-30 p.m.

AUDIN RASMUSSEN,
WATCHMAKER & JEWELLER.

Good Stock of WATCHES, CLOCKS and RINGS at reasonable prices
Give Her a Ring for Xmas —— Give Him a Watch for Xmas

283 ECCLESALL ROAD,   SHEFFIELD.

Sheffield Home Guard,   5th Battalion

" E " COMPANY

PRESENT

by kind permission of Major G. BARNSLEY, O.B.E.
(Officer Commanding "E" Coy.)

A

GRAND
CONCERT

(Compered by Mr. LAURIE LINGARD)

December 12th, 1940.

Light Refreshments during the
Interval at moderate charges.

PROGRAMME - - 2d.

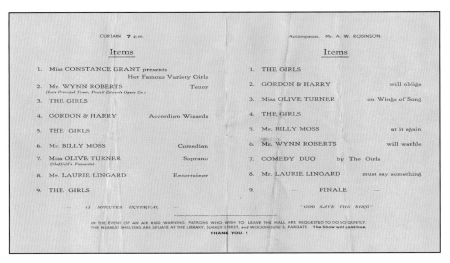

CURTAIN 7 p.m.

Accompanist. Mr. A. W. ROBINSON.

Items

1. Miss CONSTANCE GRANT presents
                      Her Famous Variety Girls
2. Mr. WYNN ROBERTS   Tenor
   (Late Principal Tenor, Powell Edwards Opera Co.)
3. THE GIRLS
4. GORDON & HARRY   Accordian Wizards
5. THE GIRLS
6. Mr. BILLY MOSS   Comedian
7. Miss OLIVE TURNER   Soprano
   (Sheffield's Favourite)
8. Mr. LAURIE LINGARD   Entertainer
9. THE GIRLS

    — 15 MINUTES INTERVAL —

Items

1. THE GIRLS
2. GORDON & HARRY   will oblige
3. Miss OLIVE TURNER   on Wings of Song
4. THE GIRLS
5. Mr. BILLY MOSS   at it again
6. Mr. WYNN ROBERTS   will warble
7. COMEDY DUO   by The Girls
8. Mr. LAURIE LINGARD   must say something
9.   —   FINALE   —

    "GOD SAVE THE KING"

IN THE EVENT OF AN AIR RAID WARNING, PATRONS WHO WISH TO LEAVE THE HALL ARE REQUESTED TO DO SO QUIETLY.
THE NEAREST SHELTERS ARE SITUATE AT THE LIBRARY, SURREY STREET, and WOODHOUSE'S, FARGATE. **The Show will continue.**
THANK YOU. !

We know from the minutes of the firm's Board Meetings that George continued to chair these and have considerable involvement in the firm. His involvement with the army continued and he was particularly involved with Army Cadets. At the works in Cornish Street there was a room where he kept items relating to this work. The photographs that follow show him at various parades and presentations. He wrote training programmes and continued to have a 'hands on' approach as deputy commander of the York and Lancaster Cadet Force from 1945-1953

Company Inspection by Brigadier A. Smith of 3rd Battalion York & Lancaster Regiment, Birdwell 20 June 1948

Below 1st Battalion York & Lancaster, Barnsley O/C Captain Sayers Presentation of medals for shooting 13 April 1951

George died on the 31st March 1958 aged 83. In the tribute in *'The Star'* he is Colonel Barnsley so sometime during the intervening years he had been promoted from major to colonel. The mourners included family and friends as well as senior staff and 40 work people from the firm. One of the friends was a Sgt. J. Thorpe and I wonder whether this was Sapper Thorpe who was part of the volunteer force who went with him to South Africa. Representatives from the army included officers from the Hallamshire Battalion York and Lancaster Regiment of the Territorial Army as well as officers from the cadet battalions.

The vast majority of Sheffield industry was represented, about 50 firms altogether, including William Jessops, Bedford and Sons. W.A Tyzack and Co. and Firth Browns. Organisations were as varied as the Methodist Youth Council and the High Speed Steel Association not to mention the Hallamshire Masonic Lodge. There is no doubt that he was a well-known, well-respected Sheffield personality. I believe the photograph and the cartoon-like drawing below show something of the man he was as he grew older. Neither is credited with an occasion and the photograph has no title. The drawing simply labelled Col. G. Barnsley O.B.E. is by a local newspaper cartoonist, Harry Heap, and appeared as No.22 in a series called '*Potted Personalities*'. (*The Star April 24 1946*).

References

(1) Malcolm John 2002 *Circles and Squares* Alison and Busby. London p.51-52

Unless otherwise stated, the original source material used in this chapter, including photographs is the possession of Colin Barnsley.

Chapter 4

Captain William Barnsley Allen VC, DSO, MC & Bar (1892 - 1933)

Name	William Barnsley ALLEN
Rank	Major
Force	Royal Army Medical Corps attd 246th Brigade Royal Field Artillery
VC	France, 3 September 1916
London Gazette	26 October 1916
Born	Sheffield, 8 June 1892
Died	27 August 1933, Bracklesham
Grave	Earnley Churchyard, Bracklesham Bay
Location of VC	Army Medical Services Museum, Aldershot

Captain William Barnsley Allen, M.C., M.B., Royal Army Medical Corps.

For most conspicuous bravery and devotion to duty.

When gun detachments were unloading H.E. ammunition from wagons which had just come up, the enemy suddenly began to shell the battery position. The first shell fell on one of the limbers, exploded the ammunition and caused several casualties.

Captain Allen saw the occurrence and at once, with utter disregard of danger, ran straight across the open, under heavy shell fire, commenced dressing the wounded, and undoubtedly by his promptness saved many of them from bleeding to death.

He was himself hit four times during the first hour by pieces of shells, one of which fractured two of his ribs, but he never even mentioned this at the time, and coolly went on with his work till the last man was dressed and safely removed.

He then went over to another battery and tended a wounded officer. It was only when this was done that he returned to his dug-out and reported his own injury.

Citation (left) from the London Gazette

117

Additional Information: Major Allen also had been awarded the Distinguished Service Order (DSO) as well as the Military Cross (MC) and Bar. He died at the age of 41 on 27th August 1933 in Bracklesham and is buried in the local churchyard.

The picture below was bought from a dealer on the internet and originally appeared in a book published during WW1 called 'Glorious Acts of Heroism'. The second picture is thought to show William at the family home in Endcliffe Vale Road, Sheffield
William was born in Sheffield on June 8th 1892 at 14 Botanical Road Sheffield. His father Percy Edwin Allen was a successful commercial traveller and his mother Edith, the daughter of Joseph Barnsley of Taptonville Crescent, Sheffield. He had an elder sister Edith who was born on 27th July 1890 and a younger sister Barbara who was born four years later on 13th September 1896. The address for the family at the time of Barbara's birth is given as 42 Southgrove Road, Ecclesall, Sheffield. I believe that it was sometime after this that the family moved to the house featured in the photo in Endcliffe Vale Road.
William was educated at what was then St Cuthbert's College, Worksop. In 1908 at the age of 17 he went to Sheffield University. He graduated with a honours degree in June 1914. During his time at the University he was awarded the Gold Medal in Pathology (1913), the Kaye Scholarship for the highest marks in physiology and anatomy and three bronze medals.
He joined the Royal Hospital as an assistant house physician but within weeks, he had enlisted with the Third West Riding Field Ambulance. In fact his date of enlistment is given in the records as 8th August 1914, four days after the outbreak of war. He was soon in France

CAPTAIN W. B. ALLEN ASSISTING MEN WOUNDED BY THE EXPLOSION OF AMMUNITION, AFTER BEING HIMSELF WOUNDED.

A German shell having exploded some ammunition which was being unloaded, causing several casualties, Captain William Barnsley Allen, M.C., M.B., of the Royal Army Medical Corps, with utter disregard of danger, ran across the open, under heavy shell-fire, and commenced dressing the wounded, thereby saving many men from bleeding to death. He was himself hit four times by pieces of shell, one of which fractured two of his ribs, but he coolly went on with his work until the last man was dressed and safely removed. For his most conspicuous bravery and devotion to duty he was awarded the V.C.

In May 1916 whilst on leave he married Mary Young, the daughter of Mr. W.Y.Mercer in Gainsborough, Lincolnshire.   In August 1916 he was awarded the Military Cross, September 3rd 1916 the VC and ten months later in June 1917 he was awarded a bar to the MC. He was invalided to England the same month. In January 1918 he was appointed acting Major but on 18th February 1918 he was transferred to the regular Royal Army Medical Corp with the rank of Captain, the rank he held at the conclusion of the war. In October 1918 he was wounded for the third time and sent back to England for the second time. This time he was awarded the D.S.O. Altogether he had served in France for three years and two months.

Little is known William's life after 1918 beyond the fact that he stayed on in the Army. There are suggestions that he divorced his first wife Mary - there is no record of her death - and married a Gertrude Craggs in 1925. A court case in July 1932 in Chichester revealed the problems that William had faced in the intervening years. He was charged as Major Allen with driving a motorcar whilst under the influence of drink. His defence stated that Major Allen had "suffered as no other man in England had suffered". He had been wounded in the chest and afterwards in the eyes. He was blind for a total of six months. In total he had been wounded seven times during the war. After the Armistice he went to India where he contracted malaria and dysentery. On his return to England the malaria and dysentery were joined by bouts of sleeping sickness and pleurisy. He took drugs and whiskey to combat these ailments and whilst he was no longer on drugs, he still took the whiskey. This defence had no effect whatsoever on the Bench; Major Allen was fined and was banned for five years (or as they put it at the time had his licence suspended).

William did not complete the ban. Thirteen months later a Dr C.R. Sadler was called by phone at 7.15 a.m. On arriving at the house he found the Major propped up in bed in accordance with the instructions he had given over the phone. He was however unconscious, blue in the face and breathing very slowly. His pupils were dilated and he had an abnormal temperature. He died within half an hour of the Doctor's arrival. In a contradiction to the evidence given in the court case a year earlier, the Doctor knew that William was still taking drugs.

An inquest was held in Chichester on 28th August 1933 presided over by the Deputy Coroner for Chichester, Mr F.B. Tompkins. Dr Sadler confirmed that William was taking drugs - veronal, opium and morphia but he had no idea of the amount he had taken. His condition on that Sunday indicated that he had overdosed with opium. The doctor confirmed that he had never heard William threaten to take his life and in his opinion was not likely to do so. The Coroner stated that he was given to understand that the Major was in the habit of taking drugs straight from the bottle without measuring the amount. In these circumstances it is quite easy to see an overdose occurring. He recorded a verdict of accidental death.

For a number of years it was thought that it was these incidents at the end of his life that was the reason why more was not known of William Barnsley Allen. He was one of the most decorated men in the First World War and time after time he displayed amazing courage and perseverance under the most testing conditions imaginable. And yet there is not even a street or building named after him. The University of Sheffield, where he had excelled, chose to ignore him in their centenary history. Needless to say there is no plaque or memorial to mark his achievements and bravery.

However the court case in June 1932 and the inquest in 1933 don't tell the whole story. An article in "Down Memory Lane" published by The Star on Monday 28th September 1987 entitled "Forgotten Hero", a rather apt title, referred to research undertaken by a doctor at the University called Dr John Lunn, who had just recently retired from the Department of Community Medicine. He pointed out that, far from being in decline after the war, William was fine. An army colleague met him on Armistice Day in Sheffield in November 1918 and recalled that William was his usual intelligent, cheery self. The following year he gave evidence in a murder case that involved the colonel of his unit who had shot and murdered a fellow officer. The Times reported that his testimony was clear and concise. It appears that he served in the Army up until 1923 and then left to go into medical practice in Hounslow, London.

Dr Lunn, firmly believes that "what did" for William Allen was "encephalitis lethargica" or to be more to the point "the sequale" or after effects of the disease.

The disease was first recognised by Arthur J Hall in 1918 who ironically was Professor of Medicine at William's old university, Sheffield. The symptoms of encephalitis lethargica, can be variable, but the illness usually starts with a high fever, headache and sore throat. Double vision, disturbance of eye movements, weakness of the upper body, tremors and strange movements, neck stiffness, intense muscle pains, a slowing of physical and mental response, drowsiness and lethargy soon follow. Unusual brain and nerve symptoms may occur, and the person's behaviour and personality may change too. Occasionally, they become psychotic with extremely disturbed thinking. Sometimes the illness is mistaken for epilepsy, hysteria or even drug or alcohol abuse. As the body shuts down, patients become increasingly sleepy and some may lose consciousness, slipping into a coma that can last months or even years. This is why the disease is sometimes known as sleeping sickness.

It is the after effects that are the most disturbing. To quote the BBC's Health Website
"the disease leaves a variety of problems that can cause prolonged disability. Most people recovering from encephalitis lethargica develop a form of Parkinson's disease, with typical symptoms of slowness, tremor and abnormal muscle movements called dystonia. As with Parkinson's there may be little facial movement, so although the person can hear, understand and is mentally fine, they don't appear to respond much to the world around them. These problems may develop as long as a year after recovery. There may also be problems with swallowing or vision, as well as long-term behavioural disorders."

William contracted the illness in 1924. How he caught it is a mystery. The court case in 1932 refers to his service in India where he contracted malaria and dysentery but even today the causes of the illness are not known. Researchers believe a virus or other type of infection may be to blame for encephalitis lethargica, but there's no good evidence that pinpoints a particular organism. A few have suggested it might be an auto-immune disease, where the body's immune system is triggered by a throat infection (perhaps with a streptococcus bacteria) that in turn attacks the nervous system. Recent research shows that areas of the brain called the mid-brain and basal ganglia become inflamed during the illness. But while anti-brain antibodies can be detected, no viruses have been found. This suggests the illness isn't caused by a virus directly entering and attacking the brain but rather indicates that the body's own immune cells are attacking the nerve cells in the brain. The condition is not curable and even today treatment is targeted at supporting the person through their illness and dealing with the symptoms as they occur.

To quote the BBC's Health Website again
"As the person recovers, physiotherapy, nutritional support and speech therapy may all help to speed them on the path back to normality. They may also need psychological support to deal with emotional and behavioural problems."
William received nothing beyond drink and drugs to cope with his illness. To be fair there is little or nothing that could have been done. The illness was very much a mystery at the time and still is. Given its variable nature, making the patient "comfortable" was the only viable option.
After posting this information to the site in October 2006 Chris Hobbs was contacted by William's family Nigel and Sue Allen who put a slightly different perspective on events leading up to William's death.

"It is also suggested in papers held (there is a wonderful file and scrapbook) at Keogh Barracks, Ash, Aldershot that his death may have been caused by his deliberately infecting himself to try to find a cure having lost patients from a similar illness. This however is only a vague suggestion and the family believe he committed suicide knowing he was developing Parkinson's disease. We will probably never know the truth of it."

Additional notes
His parents PERCY EDWIN ALLEN and EDITH BARNSLEY were married in the December quarter of 1889 (PRO REF Ecclesall Bierlow Volume 9C Page 477)
Confirmation of his birth can be found in the PRO registers for the June Quarter of 1892 - ALLEN William Barnsley, Ecclesall Bierlow Vol 9C Page 455
William attended the Victoria Cross reunion dinner on Saturday, 9th November 1929 in The Royal Gallery, House of Lords, Palace of Westminster, London.
There is a list of Victoria Cross holders who loaned their awards for an Exhibition to mark the centenary of the Victoria Cross at Marlborough House, London, from the 15th of June to the 7th of July 1956. William's VC was one of the awards exhibited and was loaned to the event by the "Societe Jersiaise, St Helier".

William's Victoria Cross is now on public display in the Army Medical Services Museum. In the article "Forgotten Hero" published by The Star in Monday 28th September 1987 the writer states that William's VC was on display at the TA Norbury Centre in Barnsley Road Sheffield.
In November 2006 I was informed that whilst at Sheffield University William was a member of the Officer's Training Corps, and is still honoured today there. Just off the main Mess in the Somme Barracks in West Street Sheffield there is an ante-room named the "Allen VC Room" which proudly displays on the wall a framed photograph of William, along with the citation as well as a copy of his VC and several of his other medals.
The RAMC museum has a wonderful display, not only of the VC, but also of his other medals, presentation platter (wedding) and photos. The scrapbook mentioned holds many army memorabilia.

William's Obituary appeared in The Times dated 29th August 1933 under the heading
V. C. DOCTOR FOUND DEAD BRAVERY ON THE SOMME. Although much of the information is cited above I have included the orbitury as written in 'The Times'

'Major William Barnsley Allen, V.C., D.S.O., M.C. and bar, late R.A.M.C., of Bracklesham Bay, Sussex, was found dead in his bedroom on Sunday. Major Allen, who was 41, was awarded the V.C. for most conspicuous bravery and devotion to duty at Mesnil, on the Somme, on September 3, 1916. The Gazette states:- "When gun detachments were unloading high explosive ammunition from wagons which had just come up, the enemy suddenly began to shell the battery position. The first shell fell on one of the limbers, exploded the ammunition, and caused several casualties. Captain Allen saw the occurrence, and at once, with utter disregard of danger, ran straight across the open, under heavy shellfire, commenced dressing the wounded, and undoubtedly by his promptness saved many of them from bleeding to death. He was himself hit four times during the first hour by pieces of shells, one of which fractured two of his ribs, but he never even mentioned this at the time, and coolly went on with his work till the last man was dressed and safely removed. He then went over to another battery and tended a wounded officer. It was only when this was done that he returned to the dugout and reported his own injury."

Major Allen was born at Sheffield on June 8. 1892, and was educated at Worksop College and Sheffield University. He gained the gold medal for pathology in 1913, and three other medals and the Kaye scholarship. He joined the Army four days after the outbreak of the War. He married at Gainsborough in May, 1916, Mary Young, daughter of Mr. W. Y. Mercer, of Gainsborough, and in the following August won the M. C. In July, 1917, Captain Allen was awarded a bar to the M. C. and was invalided to England in the same month. In January 1918, he was made acting major, and in October was wounded for the third time and invalided for the second time to England and awarded the D. S. O. He had served in France three years and two months and was transferred to the Regular R.A.M.C. in February 1918, as a captain the rank which he held at the conclusion of the War. When in July last year* (1932) Major Allen was charged at Chichester with driving a motorcar while under the influence of drink it was stated on his behalf that he had suffered as no other man in England had suffered. He was wounded in the chest, and afterwards in the eyes, being blind for six months. Altogether he was wounded seven times. When the War ended he went to India, where he contracted malaria and dysentery. Returning to England he gradually recovered, but later suffered from sleeping sickness malaria, dysentery, and pleurisy. Because of sleeplessness he began taking whisky and later drugs. He was able to throw off drugs, but still took whisky. The Bench fined Major Allen, and suspended his licence for five years.

In January this year it was announced in the London Gazette: " Major Allen, Royal Army Medical Corps, ceased to belong to the Reserve of Officers on account of ill-health." At the inquest held yesterday by the Deputy Coroner for Chichester (Mr. F. B. Tompkins) a verdict was recorded that death was due to an overdose of opium by misadventure. Dr. C. R. Sadler said that he was called by telephone about 7.15 on Sunday morning. He found the major propped up in bed, in accordance with instructions he had given over the telephone. He was blue in the face, absolutely unconscious, and his breathing very slow. His pupils were contracted and his temperature abnormal. He died about half an hour later. The witness knew that Major Allen took drugs - veronal, opium and morphia -but he had no idea of the quantity he used. He knew from his condition on Sunday that it must have been a fairly large amount. Death was due to opium poisoning. He had never heard the Major threaten to take his life, and in his opinion he was not a person who was likely to do so. Dr. Sadler mentioned that Mrs. Allen was not at home at the time, being ill in a nursing home. , The Coroner said that he was given to understand that Major Allen had been in the habit of taking drugs from a bottle without measuring the dose. One could quite imagine how possible it would be for an overdose to be taken in such circumstances. In his opinion it was accidental.'

He is buried in Earnley Churchyard, Bracklesham Bay in West Sussex. He was 41 years old. The pictures of the grave and headstone were taken in 2008.

References

Cited by Chris Hobbs http://www.chrishobbs.com/williamallen1916.htm:
The London Gazette 1916
The Times dated 1931 - 1932
The Times dated 29th August 1933
BBC's Health Website
Down Memory Lane" published by *The Star* in Monday 28th September 1987 - "Forgotten Hero''.

Chapter 5

George Barnsley, 1875-1915

This particular George Barnsley is another family mystery man. In many ways he is representative of so many young men of his generation and class. He is the grandson of his namesake who was a highly successful self-made entrepreneur of the 19th century industrial revolution. The grandfather, George (1810-1879) would have known great poverty as a child, as an apprentice file maker and even in his early years when he finished his apprenticeship. We know his father, died before he reached an age to be taken on as an apprentice so there would have been no financial support from his father. Even Joseph, (1842-1888) this young George's father, would in his early years have lived in cramped conditions and most probably learnt a trade until such time as his father, George Barnsley (1810-1879), made enough money for them to move to a house in a better district.

Young George, born in 1875 was the third child but first son born into a family who over the previous few years would have seen a huge leap forward in their standard of living. His father, Joseph had married Emma Harrap in 1862 and it seems possible that her father was a manager in the Barnsley family firm. Young George therefore from birth had all the material advantages that the two previous generations had not known until their adulthood. However, modern child psychologists would see him as having something of an emotionally deprived childhood and adolescence. His mother died when he was 10 years old and his father 3 years later in 1888. In addition his father would have spent a considerable amount of time away from home travelling on behalf of the firm. In 1861 the census shows Joseph as being at the Red Lion in Birmingham and in 1871 he does not appear on the census. Colin Barnsley has a picture of Joseph with a customer in Germany so he must have done trips overseas to promote the firm's tools and this is possibly where he was in 1871.

One of young George's Uncles, also George, (1837-1895) was his guardian under the terms of Joseph's will (along with his two other executors, Samuel Brown, Joseph's brother-in-law and Henry Whitehall Brierley) though the family had lived in 1881 next door in Oxford Street to another uncle, Joseph's brother Arthur. Sadly though, Arthur was to die in 1889 only a year or so after Joseph's death. Uncle George had no children and in fact died in 1895 just before young George gained his majority and Uncle Henry was widowed twice by 1881. This young man was certainly surrounded by grief in his early years and also saw the death of cousins as babies or young children. Again he may have been representative of his time in this respect.

In 1891 he was at a boarding school, Trinity College in Harrogate, the fees for which were no doubt paid from the interest on £7000 left in trust for him from his father's estate and which would become his when he reached the age of majority. George and his two sisters were the chief beneficiaries of the estate. At the time of Joseph's death this was about £11,000. This equates to about 1 million pounds at today's values.

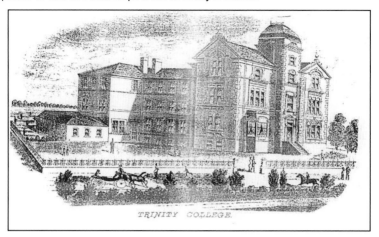

TRINITY COLLEGE.

Trinity College

Trinity College Harrogate had been opened in purpose-built buildings in 1881. The builder was Mr H Downes. It was in Park Avenue in the West End Park area of the town not very far from 'the Stray'. The advertisement placed in the Harrogate Advertiser 14th January 1882 reads as follows:
High Harrogate College
Mr J P Hughes
Begs to announce that he has moved to the handsome and commodious building - Trinity College, Which has been erected for him in the West End Park, Harrogate The schoolroom, dining hall, and class rooms, are spacious and lofty, the dormitories numerous and well- ventilated, and all are heated with hot water. Among the advantages the boys will enjoy are a large swimming bath, a lawn tennis ground, fives court, covered playground and gymnasium, cricket field, &c.
The great successes that have been achieved by the pupils of High Harrogate College in examinations and in field sports are a guarantee of the attention paid by the Head Master to the mental and physical training of his boys.
Arrangements have been made by which pupils whose friends desire it may pass any length of time that may be required at a school in Germany without any extra charge beyond travelling expenses, and remain whilst there under the supervision of Mr Hughes.
References to parents of pupils. Prospectuses on application. Day Boys on Inclusive Terms.(1)

The college had an open day in July 1881. This was reported on in both the Harrogate Herald and in the Advertiser (2).
In 1939 there appeared in the Harrogate Herald (3) a feature 'Recollections of a former pupil, Trinity College. The writer W.H. Bettis had started at the

126

school in 1886 which would almost certainly make him contemporary with George Barnsley. He writes:

We had a large gymnasium and swimming bath and a certain Professor Lacon used to come from Leeds once a week to teach swimming and gymnastics. I was scared of him and thought him rather hard hearted as he used whilst teaching swimming with a belt apparatus to slacken the rope and let the boy go under if not pleased with his progress. It happened to me many times. The same-as I thought at the time-rather harsh treatment was carried out in the gymnasium but maybe it did us good in the long run.
We had the privilege of riding our bikes round and round a small park which was opposite the school gates. This was of course the penny-farthing variety and not the safety bike of to-day.
We played cricket, football and a game called 'wyley' in which only one goal post was used. We also had tennis courts but I am afraid the standard of our tennis was very different from what it is today. Cricket was my special forte. I was in the first eleven and enjoyed the game immensely. If I remember aright the County ground at Harrogate ajoined the school ground, and we used to borrow their roller for our pitch...We used to have very pleasant outings during the term to places like Brimham Rocks and Bolton Abbey and I remember the more daring of the boys jumping the Strid then.

The sporting facilities and out of door activities reflect the public school beliefs of that time of 'a healthy mind in a healthy body' reinforced by theories about the survival of the fittest which have their roots in Darwinism. In addition it was firmly believed that team games fostered team spirit and unselfishness.

In the advert on the previous page mention is made of the possibility of boys spending time in Germany and I do wonder whether the young George spent any time in Germany given that his father's business had taken him there. If he had been expected to go into the family firm and continue business with customers in Germany this may have been one reason for the choice of this particular school.

When Mr Hughes' death was reported in the Harrogate Herald of 25th November 1908, it was said that at one time the annual sports of Trinity College had been one of Harrogate's season events and attracted quite a fashionable gathering.

The next 10 years

The next trace of George is contained in a land registry document. A deed was made between Henry Barnsley of 2 Newbould Road, Sheffield, and of Cornish Works, steel and file manufacturer and Walter Thomas Carr (Henry's brother-in-law, married to Annie, Henry's sister) of 4 Southbourne Road, Sheffield, commercial traveller (the Vendors) who conveyed the entire property (shaded pink) to George Barnsley of 24 Crownhill Rd, Harlesden, Middlesex (1887 volume 17 page 13 entry 7 registered 27th April 1897). In August 1899 George still at the same address sold the premises back to Henry Barnsley by registered deed. (1899 volume 35 page 321 entry 141 registered August 19th 1899). A retired accountant we consulted has suggested that if there was any threat to the business at the time, transferring the ownership of the buildings out of the hands of the directors would have kept the buildings in the family ownership even if everything else had been lost as a consequence of bankruptcy proceedings.

There is no specific information so far as I am aware concerning the firm of George Barnsley and Sons but in the 1890s Sheffield producers faced severe competition and increasingly felt the impact of tariffs in foreign markets. W.H. Brittain, the president of the Chamber of Commerce, warned readers of the 'Sheffield Daily Telegraph' in 1894:
In this time of high tariffs when walls were built up against us in certain markets…we should do our best to hold our own…and seek fresh outlets in every direction we could possibly extend our commerce. (4).
A Royal Commission in the mid 1880s heard James Willis Dixon report on behalf of Sheffield Businesses in the light trades that high tariffs in the United States, Canada, France, Spain and Russia were hampering development of new lines of trade. Between 1890-1894 the economy suffered a severe recession. Exports fell16% and industrial production 6%(5). All this would strongly support the theory that the firm's directors were indeed taking steps to protect family wealth if the firm did go bankrupt during the recession.

According to the 1901 census it would appear that George, then aged 26 had taken himself to a private clinic in Little Aston, Shenstone, four miles south of Lichfield. According to Kelly's directory for Staffordshire 1900, Little Aston Hall had been converted in 1898 into a private home for 'Inebriates' with accommodation for 21 patients.

Sadly there was no more information of George's whereabouts until 1914 when he enlisted in Middlesex in the 2nd battalion Royal Dublin Fusiliers. His birthplace as well as his residence is given as Sheffield. It seems surprising that he didn't enlist in Sheffield as his cousin also George Barnsley was in the team of recruitment officers there. On the other hand since he joined the ranks he may not have wanted to meet face to face with his cousin; perhaps Middlesex was, for him, a more congenial option. He does not appear anywhere on the 1911 census as far as I can discover. There is one other family link to Middlesex. In 1932, Edith Dorothy Allen who was George's niece was living in Hampton Hill though George had in fact died many years previous to this date. We know of Edith's address from a land registry document in which she was sold properties (situated in Sheffield) by Major George Barnsley and a Henry Austin Palmer who like Edith lived in Middlesex. Theses comprised a factory, six houses, a public house and a beer house.

World War 1

The Royal Dublin Fusiliers were then a part of the British Army and although substantially made up of Irishmen there were many English-born men in their ranks. They were dispatched to France in August 1914 as part of the British Expeditionary force and landed at Boulogne on the 22nd.

On April 23rd they left Bailleul at 7.30 in the evening and marched north. After billeting for the night at Westoutre they arrived towards the end of the day on the outskirts of Ypres in Belgium. The engagement that they were involved in was the Battle of St Julien, which became known later as the Second Battle of Ypres. The whole area was honeycombed with trenches and strewn with barbed wire. The Canadians were still holding St Julien. They had been driven left by a gas attack. The Royal Dublin Fusiliers were in range of the German machine guns and took heavy casualties one of whom was George Barnsley. He was killed in action 24th April 1915, the first day of the engagement, which continued until May 25th.

His death is recorded on the Menin Gate Memorial in Belgium. (6) There is a discrepancy in the dates in that in Army records he died, April 24th 1915 though his date of death is recorded on the Gate as May 24th. I believe the April date to be correct, working from the battle dates.

BARNSLEY, GEORGE	
Initials:	G
Nationality:	United Kingdom
Rank:	Lance Corporal
Regiment/Service:	Royal Dublin Fusiliers
Unit Text:	2nd Bn
Age:	40
Date of Death:	24/05/1915
Service No:	16344
Additional information:	Son of the late Joseph and Emma Barnsley
Casualty Type:	Commonwealth War Dead
Grave/Memorial Reference:	Panel 44 and 46
Memorial:	**YPRES (MENIN GATE) MEMORIAL** www.cwgc.org/search/cemetery_details.aspx?cemetery=91800&mode=1

In Memory of
Lance Corporal GEORGE BARNSLEY

16344, 2nd Bn., Royal Dublin Fusiliers
who died age 40
on 24 May 1915
Son of the late Joseph and Emma Barnsley.
Remembered with honour
YPRES (MENIN GATE) MEMORIAL

Commemorated in perpetuity by
the Commonwealth War Graves Commission

www.cwgc.org/search/certificate.aspx?casualty=926741

George was a young man whose life was shortened by war and in this he is again representative of his generation, thousands of whom died in France or Belgium between 1914-18. The picture on the next page portrays the horror of trench warfare.

References

(1) *Harrogate Advertiser* 14th January 1882
(2) Ibid 9th July 1881
(3) *Harrogate Herald* 23rd Aug 1939
(4) Quoted in Binfield C et al editors *The History of the City of Sheffield 1843-1993* Vol. 2 *'Society'*, Sheffield Academic Press pp217-218
(5) Ibid p220

Chapter 6

Eugene Leclere 1901-1982

In the autumn of 2005 I decided to clear out a suitcase full of old photographs and other small 'treasures' that had come from my mother who had died in 2003. One of the items turned out to be a Christmas card to my parents from 'Aunty Lily' and inside it was a little card which said: *with love and best wishes for your future happiness from Aunty Lily.* (*See* the little card superimposed on the Christmas card back below). On the back of the card was her name and address Mrs L. Leclere, 174 Devonshire St. Sheffield. Until this discovery I had never known her surname after marriage or where exactly she had lived.

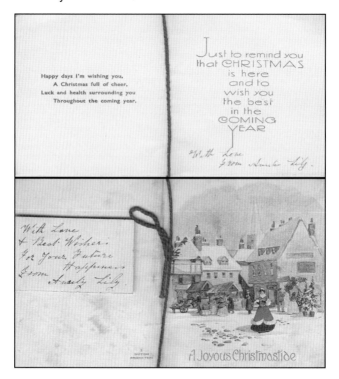

I believe this small card accompanied a wedding present for my parent's marriage in 1939. My parents had mentioned from time to time that Aunty Lily who was my paternal grandmother's older sister had died In the Sheffield Blitz on 12th Dec 1940, together with two young relatives, Doris Leclere aged 13 and Eileen Leclere aged 10. Lily's mother was *Elizabeth Barnsley*. I knew that Eugene lived in Gosport Hampshire and that he had sent his children to Sheffield because he believed that it would be a safer place than Gosport. The whole story to a child in the 1950s was strange because Eugene was always referred to as Cousin 'Gene' which I registered as a girl's name as I never saw it written down. I also recall that when my parents went on a cruise in the 1960s they went to see him on their way to Southampton. I think in the vagueness of childhood memories I had thought that Lily was Cousin Gene's wife.

I did find a list of civilian war-dead and this confirmed the names of the three. I then consulted the civilian war-dead roll of honour in Sheffield Local Studies Library which gave more detail stating that the children were daughters of Mr. E. Leclere of 79 Queen's Rd, Gosport and giving their ages as Doris aged 13, Eileen aged 10 and that Lily was aged 66. I immediately had a problem with Lily's age. There was no way she could be the girls' mother. She proved to be their grandmother widow of Marcelline Leon Leclere the son of Henri Leclere, a French immigrant who was a silversmith. He had married and settled in Sheffield and from him and his sons grew the small firm of Leclere Silversmiths, which were situated next to the Globe Inn in Howard Street. The spoon bowl shows the 'EL' on the left, which was their mark. (EL was the initial of the eldest son). However Marcelline, Lily's husband followed his mother's trade and became a master baker.

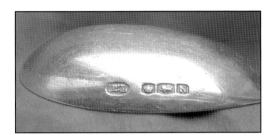

Cousin 'Gene'

The family story is that Eugene an engineer ran away from home in Sheffield to join the Royal Navy. He was married at Alverstoke Church in Hampshire in 1924 when he would have been 23 years old. His wife was Lily Eileen McGlead. All their children were registered as being born in Alverstoke. Marie the eldest child died as an infant the same year that Leon the second child was born. Eileen's birth certificate states that Eugene was a stoker petty officer on HMS Serepis

The following description of Alverstoke (probably dates from early 1900s) from the Genuki website, reveals why it might have seemed sensible in 1940 to send the children to live in Sheffield. The locality would have been facing the double threat of enemy bombing as well as invasion:

Alverstoke, a village, a parish, and a liberty in Hants. The village stands adjacent to Stoke Bay station on the L. & S.W.R., opposite Spithead, 1 3/4 mile SSW of Gosport. It is a pleasant place, with charming environs. The parish includes also the town of Gosport... the Royal Marine Barracks, the Haslar Barracks, the Royal Naval Hospital,

Blockhouse Fort, and Forts Rowner, Gomer, Brockhurst, Monckton, and Grange. Acreage, 3783, of which 1223 are water and foreshore; population of the civil parish, 25,452.... Many excellent mansions, villas, and other residences, with gardens and terraces, adorn the surface and the shores, and a rich extensive prospect is enjoyed of the Solent and the Isle of Wight. Stoke Bay is now a noted roadstead, where all the steam war-ships when newly fitted with their engines test their speed at the measured mile.

The photograph is of the Solent and Isle of Wight from Stokes Bay in September 2007. The portrait is believed to be Eugene Leclere when a young man.

The 4th *HMS Serapis* was a destroyer launched in 1918, sold 1934. A 5th was launched in 1943 and broken up 1962

He survived the war which given the tragedy of his daughters seems almost ironic. Lily Eileen Leclere (Gene's wife) died in Worthing in 1988 aged 84. Eugene died six years before his wife in August 1982 when they were still living in St. Andrews Road Gosport. He finished his career as a Chief Petty Officer.

From September 1936 to July 1939 Gene was serving on HMS Hood sailing the Mediterranean during the Spanish civil war. He was posted in October 1939 to HMS Wessex. In May 1941, the Bismarck, sank HMS Hood. Eugene's posting had saved his life. There were 1,421 crew on board HMS Hood and only three survived, They were Able Seaman Ted Briggs, Able Seaman Robert Tilman and Midshipman William Dundas. Leon, Eugene's son, can remember being outside Cockaynes' Department Store in Sheffield waiting for a tram when the shocking news of the sinking of the Hood was rumoured through the queue.

Gene's posting to serve on the Wessex involved spending some time patrolling the English Channel and the ship was involved in skirmishes near Calais early in WW2. Together with *HMS Vimiera* and a Polish destroyer, the *Burza*, they had been ordered to shell German positions. They opened fire on an enemy armoured column at Sangate Hill, west of Calais. Just ten minutes later 27 German planes attacked and sank the Wessex. The two other vessels escaped, though both were damaged. One German plane was shot down. Gene survived. However according to his son, Leon, it was this experience that convinced him that it would be a good idea to send his children to what he thought would be a place of greater safety with his Cousin Fred and his wife Pat who lived in Sheffield. Eugene's mother and Fred's mother were sisters. Lily had married Marcelline Leon Leclere and Sarah married Jim Ashton. My grandmother Eliza was their younger sister who had married Albert Edward Bell. Fred and Pat lived in Fulwood, which was and still is a very leafy and attractive Sheffield suburb. In the autumn of 1940 Pat was taken ill and went into hospital so Leon went to stay with the Ashton's and the two girls went to Lily who had been widowed some years previously though she had continued to keep the baker's shop in Devonshire Street which was also her home. All the children were due to return to Fred and Pat on December 13th. This was not to be. On December 12th 1940 Sheffield experienced the worst night of the Blitz. This is an account given by one of Sheffield's leading historians:

The main attack came on the night of Thursday 12 / Friday 13 December t940. A nearly full moon and a crisp frost ensured good visibility over most of the city, but ground fog shrouded Attercliffe and Rotherham and obscured the steelworks. The first of 336 German bombers flew in from the south at 7 p.m. They came down the Sheaf Valley, dropping incendiaries and small high-explosive bombs, to form a huge ring of fire. Between 10.38 p.m. and 2.15 a.m. the raid was intense. The blitz on the city centre began around 11 p.m. Terrible damage was inflicted on The Moor, then on High Street , Commercial Street, Haymarket, Exchange Street and Campo Lane. At 11.35 pm.a large explosion announced the destruction of the Neepsend gasworks. Ten minutes later, the Marples Hotel was hit and 70 people were killed in the cellar in what turned out to be the worst incident of the raid. The fracturing of water mains severely hampered the efforts of the firemen so fires in the city centre quickly got out of control. Every building in Angel Street and King Street was either bombed or on fire. C&A's, Walsh's, Burton's, and Sheffield's other major shops in High Street and The Moor were devastated, but those in Fargate and Pinstone Street escaped. The last bomber departed at 3.50 a.m., and at 4.17 a.m. the all--clear was sounded. The Luftwaffe returned home without losses. They had destroyed much of the city centre arid had inflicted heavy damage on an area bounded by Millhouses, Meersbrook, Heeley, Norfolk Park, Park Hill, Pitsmoor, Neepsend, Glossop Road, Broomhill, Sharrow and Nether Edge. Water, gas, electricity, and transport services were seriously disrupted, but the industrial east end had escaped.
German bombers returned three days later. This time their target was the steelworks. At 6.50 pm. on Sunday 15 December the first of 94 aircraft reached the Prince of' Wales Road. They dropped their bombs with considerable effect until 10.05 pm. A rolling mill at Brown Bayley's was

completely destroyed and two others were damaged. Other works suffered to a lesser degree. Incendiary bombs did a great deal of carnage in Attercliffe. Ten people were killed in Coleford Road and many more were made homeless. Christ Church was burnt out and never rebuilt.

In these two raids 2,906 houses and shops were destroyed or damaged beyond repair. Altogether, 82,413 buildings were affected in one way or another, though many of them merely suffered broken windows. Precise casualty figures are hard to establish because accounts vary. The official History of Civil Defence (1955) records 589 killed and 488 seriously injured. Further attacks were feared, but the Germans began to blitz Manchester, Liverpool and Derby instead. After 1940 the only bombs dropped on Sheffield were those jettisoned by isolated aircraft. Weather conditions probably saved the city on two later occasions.

(Taken from David Hey *A History of Sheffield* Carnegie Publishing 271-272).

Following the Sheffield Blitz in December 1940 Devonshire Street in Sheffield looked like this:

Eugene, then based at Rosyth in Scotland, was given compassionate leave and came to Sheffield. He dug his mother and two daughters out of the rubble with his bare hands. After the burial he returned to his ship and didn't return home for four years. At the end of WW2 when the site was cleared, Devonshire Green was created and 40 years afterwards in 1980 five trees were planted with a plaque with incised black lettering which bears the inscription:

The pictures on the following page show the Devonshire Green Memorial and below them are photographs of Lily, Doris and Eileen and the memorial stone on the communal grave in City Road Cemetery. Some of these stones which circle the wall have dropped out or been stolen including that of Lily. Also pictured is the whole communal grave.

DEVONSHIRE GREEN

This open space is dedicated to the memory of
those Citizens of Sheffield who died on the nights
of the 12th, 13th and 15th of December 1940
during aerial bombardment of the City in the
Second World War 1939-45

This stand of five trees was planted by
The Lord Mayor of Sheffield
(Councillor W. Owen J.P.)
on the 14th December 1980
to commemorate the 40th Anniversary of the Raids

EILEEN & DORIS LECLERE

IN THIS GARDEN
134 CITIZENS REST
IN A COMMUNAL
✝ GRAVE ✝
THEIR NAMES
ARE RECORDED
THEY DIED BY ENEMY ACTION
✝

My brother recalls driving along Devonshire Street with my father in the 1960s and my father telling him that Aunt Lily's baker's shop was the only building in the street to be directly hit. I believe the picture below showing all the rubble towards the left is what remained of the house and shop. It is believed that the family would have died instantly as the impact would have sucked out all the air from the shelter in the cellar. Lily, wife of Eugene, stayed in Sheffield with her son Leon for a few months and they both then returned to Gosport in the summer of 1941 and moved to a different house where Eugene and Lily lived until Eugene's death.

Meanwhile Gene now posted to HMS Queen Elizabeth had sailed in 1941 from Rosyth where Leon thinks they were doing trials. On the web I found a diary of a fellow crewmember. This gives a first-hand account of experiences that Eugene and others on board would have had during the few months following the deaths of his mother and two daughters.

HMS Queen Elizabeth with HMS Valiant
Picture courtesy of Ian Rhodes

AROUND AND ABOUT WITH HMS QUEEN ELIZABETH

The above picture described as 'the boys' was probably taken by the author of the diary or one of his shipmates. (Picture courtesy of Ian Rhodes)

March 18th 1941 *(sic)*
Leave Scapa to hunt two German Battle Cruisers trying to get back to Germany after operating in Atlantic, they are the "Scharnhorst" and "Gneisenau". No sign of them on 18th or 19th. We are at present searching at a point between Iceland and Greenland. 20th — signal from Admiralty states — HMS Ark Royal and HMS Renown are on the trail of the enemy and are 160 miles to the south of them. The position of the enemy is 900 miles south of us, us being QE and HMS Hood, we set our speed to 20 knots and head south. The enemy are also steaming at 20 knots north and are being shadowed by the "Ark's" planes. We should be in contact with enemy in less than a day. 21st — Disappointment. The enemy has eluded us aided by bad visability. 23rd — Enemy is reported to be taking refuge in Brest. We leave it to the RAF. We are back in dear old Scapa again.

April
2rd — Leave Scapa to pick up important convoy in Halifax, Canada. Two thirds of the way over and alter course to south as the Admiralty believes enemy ships in Brest are going to make a break for Germany again. Pick up HMS Repulse and proceed together toward a point off Brest.

April 8th — Repulse leaves us and heads for Gib. 10th — oil fuel running short. We are at present making circles somewhere in South Atlantic awaiting enemy movements. 11th — Leave for nearest port which is Gibraltar. 14th — Arrive at the Rock, re-fuel and re-ammunition. 15th — Leave Gib for Freetown, West Africa. 21st — Arrive Freetown, helluva hot. 24th — Leave Freetown. 30th — Back in Gib again.

May
3rd — Leave Gib for eastern Med, with HMS Ark Royal, Repulse. Have five important transports with us. 5th — Are preparing for possible air attack as we are nearing southern Sardinia and Sicily, well-known danger area. 8th — Pick up more warships sent to help us through "Narrows", the Narrows being a part where we pass within five miles of enemy coast. Our force now consists of HMS Ark Royal, Repulse, Barham, Warspite and Valiant, our escort consists of about 20 destroyers and cruisers.

9th — Are attacked by eight torpedo-carrying planes, most of the torpedoes aimed at the Ark, all miss. Later attacked by Bombers. We shoot a couple down. Attacks go on all day. Same night, the QE is singled out and attacked by one torpedo plane. Torpedo misses the ships side of stern by a few feet. The Italian news next claims a direct hit on us. Also claims to hit the Ark, in fact later claims to have destroyed half of our force. We had a good laugh while listening.

11th — The enemy have packed up their attacks as we are now well past the foot of Italy. Their attacks cost them 16 bombers. "Nice catch!"

14th — Arrive at our destination — Alexandria, Egypt. 17th — Are now patrolling off Crete to ward off any attempt made by the enemy to ship troops across to Crete where a very fierce battle is in progress. Visited by dive bombers again. We don't mind. We're used to it by now. Or are we? 24th — Back in Alex after being relieved by Warspite and Valiant which are damaged by bombs later. The aircraft carrier "Formidable" which was out with us at Crete received a direct hit on the bows with a 1000 lb bomb. In the same attack the destroyer "Nubian" is hit astern. We, the QE, as usual escape damage.

The above pictures show *HMS Queen Elizabeth* in Alexandra Harbour (left) and King George VI inspecting her crew probably at an earlier date.

The escape was not to last for long. Italian miniature submarines had penetrated the submarine screen by following surface shipping underwater, into the harbour. Unnoticed, the crews of the mini-subs had attached limpet mines to the hulls of the battleships Queen Elizabeth and Valiant. When these exploded the vessels did not sink completely, but were left sitting on the harbour bottom.

As the mine exploded Gene was leaving the engine room. He swallowed fuel oil as he was escaping which caused internal injury. He was treated in Alexandria Hospital where part of his stomach/intestine was removed. The Queen Elizabeth and the Valiant were given temporary repairs in dry dock in Alexandria. The Italian submariners who had been unable to escape, were located clinging to buoys in the harbour and taken prisoner. In less than two months the enemy had written off three battleships, and left the Eastern Mediterranean Fleet much depleted. The Fleet was left with just a handful of cruisers, destroyers, minelayers, frigates and submarines.

The above pictures are from the People's War on line archive of wartime memories contributed by members of the public and gathered by the BBC.

The archive can be found at www.bbc.co.uk/ww2peopleswar and were taken by William Wilder who was a leading stoker on *HMS Queen Elizabeth* and placed there by his grandson, John Robertson. I assume therefore that Gene as a chief petty officer stoker would have been William's senior officer. William took many pictures not only on board *HMS Queen Elizabeth* but also of other Royal Navy Ships.
.

When the ship was repaired, it sailed for South Africa and then went to America for more substantial repairs. Gene served for a while at a US naval base, Asbury Park and eventually returned to Southampton on the liner *Queen Elizabeth* which was a troop ship in 1944. He was invalided out of the Navy in 1945.

Also in the People's War archive I found an account by a survivor of this same incident in Alexandria Harbour. It sounds as though the writer's experience was similar to that of Gene. The source of this account is as for the photographs above, though the account is from Robert Simpson. (Sic)

There was a Royal Naval Fleet Club in Alex. where you could get ice cold Stella beer and where they played Tombola when the Fleet was in. Thinking now of the dear old ladies playing their Bingo at home - at the Fleet Club practically every number had a nick-name, and the numbers were also called out so rapidly that by the time the ladies picked up their pens to play - the game would have been over! For the next 18 months we took part in several more convoys and assisted in the evacuation of Crete when invaded by the Germans. The other two capital warships with us were H.M.S. Valiant and H.M.S. Barham. When en route to pick up a convoy one day the "Barham" received a direct hit amidships from three torpedoes from an Italian submarine. There was no warning and I just happened to be on the upper deck when it happened and heard someone shout out "Look at the "Barham !" and we could see she was obviously in trouble and almost stationary, then suddenly listed to starboard and even from some distance I could see some of the crew abandoning the ship then again, very suddenly she blew up and I saw one of the huge 15" Turrets, complete with its twin guns, briefly silhouetted against the sky before crashing down into the sea. In just 7 minutes she was gone. I just stood there transfixed with horror for several minutes and to this day I will never forget it. For the rest of the trip there was no sound of laughter and everything was carried out very quietly on board. Up to then we had a sort of sense of security but it had now been rudely shattered. We heard later that approximately a quarter of the crew were saved but over 600 went down with her, many of them known by our own crew. I was just passing one of the 4.5 Turrets one day when it suddenly fired although I did not recall Action Stations being sounded. The blast put my left ear out of action for about a week and I only regained partial hearing in it afterwards.

Mail from home was a rare commodity as unfortunately a high proportion got lost in transit but I treasured each letter received, at that time written on "Airgraph" reduced in size, usually written by Dad who had a very neat hand. It was so nice to get news from home as we had no idea what was happening on the home front and perhaps just as well we did not. I used to find a quiet corner and read it several times and sometimes just feel a little homesick. Round about the end of January, 1942, I was told a parcel had arrived for me. The 12inch circular package looked a bit battered but I eagerly opened it to find a mouldy birthday cake and a card – I am afraid the cake found a watery grave but I did appreciate the thought. They did not know it would take nearly 4 months to reach me ! For the whole time we were in Alex. Harbour the weather never changed, monotonous blue skies every day and I would cheerfully have given a month's pay for just one cool, wet day - still it enabled me to tan to a dark brown which stayed for quite some time after we left. One of the perks sailors enjoyed on board ship, besides their daily issue of rum, was to purchase at Duty Free prices cigarettes and tobacco from the Canteen. So for an old 6d you could have 20 Players or Senior Service and for 4d 20 Woodbines. The Boss let us have them free but in moderation. Towards the end of our stay in Alex. normal supplies began to get scarce and we had to rely a lot on local traders.

After returning off a convoy trip early one morning and as I was sleeping on the floor of the Goffer shop, I was rudely awoken by a loud bang vibrating the ship and shaking loose the large Oxygen cylinder which crashed down on my right foot. The "bang" was caused by two Italian one-man submarines breaching the harbour defences and attaching Limpit mines to our bottom hull, blowing a hole 50 ft by 30 ft causing us to settle on the sea bed. The same happened to the "Valiant" putting both ships temporarily out of action. I was taken to the 64th General Hospital in Alex. where they somehow managed to put my badly broken foot back together again - I reckoned myself very lucky it was my foot which was damaged and not my head. Whilst I was in hospital the Q.E. was put into a large floating dock where the damage was temporarily repaired and the hole covered up with a steel plate. Towards the end of my hospital stay, a small group of us were invited to the residence of the Chief of Police, very palatial in its own grounds, and given a very nice tea. Also whilst there we had a little go on the Bowling Green they had - the first game of Bowls I played. We could not manage the tennis !

Earlier during our stay in Alex. when going ashore alone shortly after we arrived, I found a very nice Greek restaurant just off Mohammed Ali square and became a regular customer. Just opposite was a stationery shop which I used occasionally and got to know the Greek owner Haig Avatis and also his pretty sister - no, I did not manage to take her out as being only 17 I did not pluck up enough courage to ask her!

The repair completed on the Q.E. the call went out for all walking wounded to return, including some from other ships in the Fleet - so with the aid of crutches I managed to get up the gangway to return to lighter duties in the Goffer shop instead of the Canteen and made sure the replaced Oxygen cylinder was very well secured! At dawn one morning in May/June, 1942, we sailed out of Alex. Harbour and proceeded through the Suez Canal en route around the Cape to Capetown. There was a recreational area with tables and chairs by the Goffer shop and some of the Royal Marine bandsmen who had been wounded used to get together some evenings and have a Jazz Session, and I used to enjoy myself using the metal draining board to beat to their rhythms.

We did not run into any trouble en route to Capetown and arrived safely with our destroyer escort. We found Capetown a beautiful place, and during our short stay there one of the residents stopped his car and took us up to the top of Table Mountain where the view was fantastic and then to his home for refreshments. On another occasion we were returning to the ship one evening when we heard some dance music and going into the dance hall we found all the dancers were coloured. Blissfully unaware whites were not welcome we
had a couple of drinks at the bar - but when I got one of the girls to dance with me I noticed one or two funny looks from the men so we decided not to dally any longer !

It was with reluctance we left Capetown to be informed we were going to Norfolk, Virginia, U.S.A. to get a proper repair done on our damaged hull and we had a practice abandoning ship routine in case we ran into rough weather across the South Atlantic and our temporary repaired plate came loose but luck was with us and we arrived safely.

Shortly after arrival I was given 10 days leave and was told arrangements had been made for me to spend it with an American family in Washington D.C. My host and hostess were Grover and Annabel Hartman who had only been married a few weeks and proved to be the most hospitable and kind people that I have ever met - in fact, we remained lifetime friends.

My stay with them was a very enjoyable experience, I was entertained in the kindest manner and sleeping in a bed again with sheets was just one of the luxuries I appreciated during my leave. Norfolk, Virginia dockyard and also ashore was a pretty rough place and with the ship crawling with workmen and constant noise, I was not unhappy when I was told I was going to be sent to a shore base on the east coast of New Jersey. I still left with mixed feelings at leaving what had been my home for over 18 months. Before I actually went to the shore base, which obviously was not quite ready, I was sent to New York to stay in a Servicemen's residence and had a nice rest there for a couple of weeks - during my stay I was invited to

spend Thanksgiving weekend with a rather wealthy American family. They celebrated it in some style and mine host introduced me to the American Highball. A generous measure of Three Roses Rye Whisky, topped up with Canadian Dry served in a very nice cut glass with ice, which I understandably acquired a taste for during my stay in the States.

Then I received instructions to travel to Asbury Park, a seaside town approximately 60 miles due south of 13 New York on the East coast in New Jersey, where I found that we had been loaned two adjacent medium sized hotels as a transit camp to provide temporary accommodation for Royal Naval personnel from the U.K. prior to them being drafted to crew the new warships being built in the U.S.A. to replace the ones we had lost on the Atlantic convoys. With the Chief there were about 6 of us to run a large Canteen and a smaller one selling stationery, souvenirs, etc. The shore base was named H.M.S. Asbury and whilst there I was promoted up to a Leading Hand (entitled to wear a hook (anchor) on my left sleeve) and a nice increase in my wages and the Chief put me in charge of the smaller stationery shop. Every two weeks a batch of personnel would arrive and be given ten dollars each straight away which the majority promptly spent on some of the approximately 20 brands of ice cream we had in stock! Having been allocated their ships they would then depart to make way for the next intake, so we were kept pretty busy. Every Tuesday evening the Chief paid for us to enjoy ourselves at the local Ten-pin bowling club. There was a very good cinema there showing previews of the latest films and the one I particularly remember was Bing Crosby in "White Christmas" and coming out feeling a bit homesick. After 18 months in the Med. I was not acclimatised to winter conditions on the exposed east coast the States and had considerable trouble trying to keep warm - I think I used at least four blankets at night! On New Years Eve, 1942, except for the Chief, we all travelled up to New York to join the celebrations. At 7p.m. precisely in Jack Dempsey's bar (a famous ex-boxer) on 42nd Street, we raised our glasses and drank to our folks back home, it being Midnight there. We then had a hectic night managing to get to Times Square in time just before Midnight, returning rather the worse for wear in the early hours of the morning to Asbury.

Petty Officer Robert (Bob) Simpson)

When Gene arrived home, he had been away for four years. In today's world that is inconceivable. He had been home a very short time when Leon was called up. In essence Leon did his National Service in the Royal Navy and spent some time in the Far East. The war in Europe was almost over. In the Far East it ended in the late summer of 1945.

The picture above on the left is of Leon with his parents Eugene and Lily about 1947 and on the right at Eugene and Lily's golden wedding anniversary.

Despite his wartime injuries Eugene lived until he was in his eighties as did Lily his wife. Given their life experiences this was, to those of us in today's world, a remarkable achievement. There seems a certain irony, given his wartime experiences spent very much on the front line where he survived several life threatening events, that he survived WW2 whilst his young daughters and his mother lost their lives as a result of enemy action.

Chapter 7

Arthur Richard Bentley 1915

Although he did not know until he was in his 90's, Arthur (born 1915) is the son of entertainer Tom Barnsley. His father died when he was a very small child so he has the name of his step-father. His family emigrated to Melbourne Australia in April 1926. School in Melbourne was a very difficult social experience, though a boy who was to remain a close friend into adulthood, Claude Henry Scriven, befriended him. Arthur reached the age of employment during the years of the great depression but eventually secured a temporary job in 'the Hill of Contentment' bookshop. Later it became permanent and was the beginning of a career in the world of books and newspapers. It was through the reading of the books and conversations with his first employer that he acquired 'an education'.

At the age of 17 in 1932 he enlisted in the 34th Fortress Company, Royal Australian Engineers (M). The 'M' was for militia as distinct from the permanent Australian forces. In 1936 Arthur married Jean Semple. Apart from the war years they were together until her death in 1997. Arthur continued with the 34th Fortress Company with weekly parades, weekend camps and rifle practice against the growing threat of a world war. During this time he also had an increasing interest in hunting all kinds of game, rabbits, hares, the occasional fox and later wallabies, kangaroos, goats and pigs. Deer became a particular interest though he didn't shoot one until after WW2. He says himself, 'It was not until years later that the ethics and philosophy of hunting were appreciated and seeped into the consciousness'.

World War 2. After discussion with Jean he enlisted in 1940 at the time that Italy joined the Axis powers some 9 months after England declared war on Germany. He joined up with his friend Claude and spent the next five and half years in the Australian Imperial Force (A.I.F.) The two friends were posted to the 3rd platoon of the 21st Anti-Tank Company at Puckapunyal about 90 kilometres north of Melbourne. They lived in galvanised wooden huts that were about 20metres by 7 metres, had wooden floors and slept about thirty men. One of the men in the platoon was Ken-von Bibra a well-known journalist with the Sun News Pictorial and a frequent customer to the bookshop. He was later killed in the Middle East. The Anti-Tank Company belonged to the 21st Brigade and their training consisted of endless digging of pits to site guns, drilling and rifle exercises.

The Middle East. They were transported to Sydney where they were ferried under the harbour bridge to HMT (His Majesty's Transport) Aquitania and sailed with HMT Queen Mary and whilst on board Arthur and Claude became part of the starboard gun crew. Their escort was HMAS Perth on which his brother in law was wireless operator. When they were within two or three days of India this escorting ship was relieved by HMS Shropshire. They docked in Bombay in November 1940 and remained for about a week

at the British Camp at Colaba before sailing in the Dutch ship SS Slamat. They disembarked at El Kantara in the Suez Canal. He writes:
'With mess tins in our hands we received a dollop of mashed potatoes, two sausages, another vegetable of some kind, a large bun and a pannikin of tea, in about as fast a time as it has taken me to write of it. El Kantara must have been the inspiration for the post-war fast food outlets.' (1) Almost as quickly they were on their way to camp at Julis near Gaza. They had the opportunity to visit the ruins of Askelon where the Queen of Sheba is reputed to have met Solomon, the Wailing Wall in Jerusalem and Tel Aviv.

1940 on the left Arthur at Julis Camp, Palestine.
1940 on the right, on day leave in Jerusalem with a friend.

At Dimra the 21st Anti-Tank Company was disbanded and the personnel absorbed into the 2/2 Tank Attack Regiment commanded by Lt. Colonel R.F. Monaghan. Arthur was soon promoted to Lance Bombardier as reconnaissance orderly and issued with a BSA motorbike. In addition he manned an antiaircraft Bren Gun. They were on the coast of the western desert 120 kilometres west of Alexandria and knew that British troops were about the same distance further west fighting the Germans under Rommel. It was during this time that Arthur and Claude had their first brush with death when they experienced an explosion of a stick of bombs just off the road ahead of them that killed 2 men and wounded others.

Syria. Shortly after this incident Lt. Colonel Monaghan was posted from 2/2 Regiment to 2/33 Battalion. After a couple of days much to Arthur's amazement the Lt. Colonel arranged for Arthur also to be transferred, and for him to be promoted to Acting Sergeant and 'Intelligence Sergeant'. Arthur was none too keen on this as it separated him from his friends and of course he knew no one in the new battalion. The British with the Free French invaded Syria in June 1941. In the ensuing fighting the Australians suffered more battle losses than in any other Middle East campaign. Most of Arthur's work was reconnaissance and then having gained the information guiding companies to the location. Sometimes he had the task of escorting prisoners of war to the 'prisoner of war cage' that was some miles away. In July 1941 after a bitter campaign, the Vichy French troops surrendered and an armistice was signed. Arthur remained in Syria until January 1942 and enjoyed the occasional day's leave in Beirut.

In February 1942 together with the rest of the 25th Brigade he boarded the American auxiliary cruiser USS Mt. Vernon for an unknown destination. The 'I' (Intelligence) Section thought, because of maps they received, that their destination was Sumatra but at Colombo those maps were withdrawn and they found themselves sailing for Freemantle where they had some shore leave before going to Adelaide. They remained here but were not allowed home leave. He along with others was about to go AWOL when he got a phone call (unheard of) from Jean who had come to Adelaide to try to meet him. They had a little time together before he was posted again to Casino in New South Wales where the 7th Division was concentrated in case of Japanese landings in North Queensland.

Papua New Guinea. This was a hugely difficult terrain where they experienced heavy rain, little sleep and food in short supply. They had to make for Iorabaiwa Ridge where three battalions of the 21st Brigade were holding the Japanese. Arthur in his memoirs quotes from William Crookes, The Footsoldiers (2) which includes this description of that first day on the Kokoda Track.

'Who will forget this "road" churned into a foot-deep morass by the passage of jeeps carrying casualties out from the trail ahead? Trucks and jeeps bogged chassis deep, had been abandoned in the mud. Each man carried five day's rations of bully beef, his share of Bren magazines, two bandoliers of ammunition (100 rounds), two four-second grenades, emergency ration and field dressing, and for those not carrying Bren magazines, a two-inch mortar bomb stuffed into the hip pocket. Although LMG numbers were carrying more weight at a given time, the average carried 55 pounds each. No thought had been given whatsoever to carrying blankets, not even one, and at this time... Our only wet weather protection was the 1908 designed groundsheet... In five hours of marching D Company was strung out for half a mile along the track. Already thirteen had fallen out... Each of us was swearing at this one mile an hour progression... By late afternoon the long muscle-jarring descent began down to the Goldie River... In two hours we climbed the short crest into the village of Uberi... where we all collapsed into exhausted rest after possibly the most gruelling twelve hours of our lives.'

Arthur was part of the advance party and he had to return to guide the remainder of the battalion to the position on the right flank of the 3rd Battalion. Arthur was with a water patrol when the Japanese penetrated the front line causing the Australians to retreat to Imita Ridge. This was the last backward move of the Australian forces during the whole campaign. It had seemed an impossible feat but some how the 14th Field Regiment got two 25-pounder artillery pieces to Uberi. The guns had been taken to pieces and their barrels shortened. These weapons helped the Australians regain Iorabaiwa.

At this point Arthur became ill with suppurating arthritis that involved him having his leg in a brace. He also had malaria and spent some time at a casualty clearing station. When he considered himself sufficiently well to return to his unit, he was not allowed to do so. He therefore with three colleagues decided to try to 'escape' to rejoin their unit under their own steam. However they were eventually 'caught' and arrested and returned to the transit deport. They opted for the charge to be heard by their own commanding officer. He all but commended them for their action!

Back to Australia. In January 1943 Arthur returned to Australia where he had seven days leave. He remained in Australia having been selected for officer training. He was sent to Woodside to the Officer Cadet Training School for the three months Number 4 course. At the end of the course he received a commission with the rank of lieutenant and was posted as an instructor to the School of Jungle Warfare in Canungra in Queensland.

New Guinea for the second time. He was posted to the 2/8th Australian Infantry Battalion, 19th Brigade in the Sixth Division located on the Atherton Tablelands. The Sixth Division sailed in November 1944 in the Liberty ship USS Thomas Corwin for New Guinea where they took over from American forces which had moved on to the Philippines. The task of the Australian Forces was to eliminate the Japanese in the Aitape-/ Wewak area. In his role as an Intelligence Officer he was called upon together with the Company Commanders to do an aerial reconnaissance. He flew with the crew of a Beaufort bomber making air strikes on targets in the Wewak area. During the flight the plane bounced and shuddered momentarily. This the crew identified as 'ack ack'. They also attempted to bomb a well-used bridge.

During the next eleven months, until the Japanese surrender in August 1945, the task involved continuous patrolling and many sharp encounters. These patrols in the steep and difficult terrain and terrible weather were always challenging though vital to the success of the campaign. On one occasion at least there was a sudden and devastating flood caused by a torrential downpour. They were in the area of the Danmap River. Members of C Company and the machine gunners were crossing to and from an island in the river when quite suddenly the river became impassable. All attempts to get a line to the men on the island failed. Although it seems that the twelve missing men survived they were rescued in daylight at sea, clinging to trees and other debris. One man was bitten in the chest by a snake. He lacerated the bite with signal wire he found attached to the log.

Trees they had climbed had got uprooted. Arthur himself on the same night lost his signet ring as he was getting his gear out of the torrent but managed later to find his sodden paybook caught in a tree ten feet above ground.

Shortly after this incident on June 11th 1945 Arthur's war came to an end. The company he was with was making an attack on an enemy stronghold near a feature known as Hill One. An air attack had already been launched followed by an artillery bombardment. The first shells fired had delayed fuses which allowed them to penetrate the ground before exploding to destroy the earthwork defences. After this there followed a bombardment of shells with instantaneous fuses intended for the enemy who had left their earthwork cover. As Arthur and a colleague were on the ground with the shells being fired over them the shells began to be touched off as they caught the foliage above their heads. Arthur had just registered their danger when he experienced an enormous physical shock. He had been hit in the head and right upper arm. The phone line to the guns had been cut so the bombardment ran its course whilst they withdrew several yards. The battalion stretcher-bearers from the indigenous population came under small arms fire as they were carrying him to the Casualty Clearing Station. The company's attack went in and the position was taken. Arthur wrote: *At one time or another I had been under fire from representatives of all the then enemies of the king, but finally two months before Japan's surrender, it was our own artillery that brought my active participation in the war to an end!*

These pictures of Arthur's arrival at the 'jeep head' after being hit by shrapnel were taken by another soldier and sent to Arthur after the war. Cameras were not allowed.

From the Casualty Clearing Station at Wewak he was flown to the 2/11th Australian General Hospital at Aitape. When discharged he flew in one of the famous biscuit bombers to Port Moresby and from there to Townsville in a Sunderland Flying Boat. Whilst he was at the Townsville staging camp the atomic bomb was dropped on Hiroshima and on Nagasaki a few days later. These are Arthur's concluding words in the section of his book on the war years:

There was no thought whatsoever for the victims, they were the enemy who, collectively had brought untold tragedy, grief and fear to millions of people. It seems not to be generally known that before the first atomic bomb was dropped, the Japanese had been given a list of twenty-four cities that would be destroyed if they did not surrender. We realised that the destruction of these two cities signalled the end of the war. Thought for the victims came later with younger generations as communal memory faded with the years.

Understandably, very few people today are able to appreciate the overwhelming feeling of relief of those who were directly affected by the war. The burden of fear, mostly hidden but ever-present and apprehension was immediately lifted from the hearts of families and loved ones in the services. Today those feelings of relief live only in the memory of the few of us left who were involved.

Arthur's service as a fulltime officer ended on the 8th November 1945.

Deer conservation. When writing his memoirs Arthur commented that the most satisfying decades of his adult life were between 1960 and 1980 when he was between 45 and 65 years of age. It was during that time that the Victorian Deer Conservation Cooperative Ltd (VDCC) had its herd of fallow deer in the enclosures of Exford road at Melton. In the next few years various organisations were formed which furthered the management and conservation of deer culminating in 1978 in the Australian Deer Research deer in the enclosures of Exford road at Melton. In the next few years various organisations were formed which furthered the management and conservation of deer culminating in 1978 in the Australian Deer Research Foundation Ltd. In a personal communication to me he said:

Always interested in wildlife, I first became interested in Australia's introduced deer in 1937 after I saw reference to the sambar in a newspaper. I must have been born a hunter - after all hunting is a cultural imperative of mankind. So from rabbits I 'graduated' to deer! Deer, being an introduced species, have been neglected by naturalists and wildlife authorities virtually since their naturalization, so after some years of untutored research I published the first book on Australia's deer in 1967. Three editions have been published, all royalties supporting research and anagement projects because deer remain a major interest.

The book is called, '*An Introduction to the Deer of Australia.*'

In his memoirs he describes how in the early days, he experimented to find some way of producing a tranquilliser dart. He first of all modified a Crossman airgun and identified that a suitable drug was 'nicotine salicilate'. The real challenge was the dart. Eventually he used an eighth of an inch twist drill fitted with a plastic cotton tail and the brass point of a Biro pen soldered to the drill for easier penetration of deer tissue. After several abortive attempts cotton wool wound into the drill grooves and held in place by a light winding of cotton threads would carry the drug. The loaded dart as carried in a small glass phial until needed. Persistence and tenacity had paid off. ———

In 1975 along with his wife Jean, he made a trip to England. This was partly to consult with and meet others involved in deer management work. One of these contacts was the renowned English authority the late Kenneth Whitehead who had a private museum of items connected with deer. In Arthur's opinion this was probably the best collection of such items in the world. It is now housed at Durham University and is known as the Whitehead Collection. (Durham University Library, Archives and Special Collections)

It was whilst Arthur was in the Lake District that news arrived that he had been awarded the British Empire Medal in the Queen's Birthday Honours for work associated with the conservation of deer.

Left Arthur in 1993 at a ceremony in which a bronze plaque was positioned to commemorate the release of sambar deer at that location in 1865. In the middle Arthur at a camp in Tasmania in 1978 having his lunch and on the right with the frog that croaked all night but was not located until daylight!

References

(1)*Their Washing Day is Monday, Memoirs of Arthur Richard Bentley* Privately published Croydon, Australia 31/7/2003
(2) quoted in Ibid

Conclusion

There are many ways in which the Barnsley family of Sheffield is typical of any family that can trace a history that spans almost five centuries. Like all families they have been influenced by local events and national politics. In earlier centuries they rented land and property from the local Lord of the Manor; some bought land and built on it; others bought property and rented out; some, particularly in the last century or two, moved away to other parts of England and to different parts of the world. We know of Barnsley descendents in Canada and Australia.

Whether they stayed or went, all were affected by national events such as the industrial revolution, economic depressions or recessions and wars and rumours of wars. Some served in the armed forces whilst others contributed to the wars through their involvement in local industry. All faced wartime deprivation and in the 20th century even civilians were at risk of their lives. Virtually every family in this century was touched by the death or injury of someone they knew or who was close to them.

All Sheffield cutlery firms have been affected since WW1 by changing trading conditions which include the imposition of import duty by countries like the old Commonwealth and the USA as well as by cheaper production costs in Asian countries. This has led to the outsourcing of some of the earlier stages of cutlery-making or to the importing of finished products. A consequence has been the shrinking of workforces and the closure of many firms. Sadly the original George Barnsley firm had this in common with so many others and finally closed at the end of 2003.

In one respect, though, the Barnsley family is different from most other families. It is possible to tell from wills that they were working metal probably to make cutting tools for use in working the land as early as the 16th century. In the 17th century they were known as cutlers and a whole succession of Barnsleys through the years appear in the records of the Hallamshire Cutlers' Company. This involvement in the trade led to the foundation of the firm that became known all over the world as George Barnsley and Sons, toolmakers. I have asked cobblers and bookbinders in shops and working museums in different parts of England if they have Barnsley tools and always they have at least one knife that is still in regular use. Colin Barnsley's firm, Woodware Repetitions now owns the name of George Barnsley and Sons and they continue this long tradition of tool making including those for leather workers into the second decade of the new millennium.